Shotguns +
Clay Target
SPORTS

TRIVIA Q + A

Also by Mike McGuire

1001 U.S. Geography Trivia Q & A

500 Ohio State Football Trivia Q & A

800 Ohio State Football Trivia Q & A

1220 Ohio State Football Trivia Q & A

500 Heisman Football Trivia Q & A

The Majors Golf Trivia Q & A

Shotguns + Clay Target Sports
Trivia Q+A
by Mike McGuire

978-0-9772661-6-6

FIRST EDITION

Published by Mike McGuire

Order copies from
Mike McGuire
27081 N. 96th Way
Scottsdale, AZ 85262-8441
(480) 563-1424

Printed in the United States of America

DEDICATION

When writing this book, one of the major motivating principles was remembering all the great times I have had over the years with my shooting buddies. I always enjoyed sitting around the open stone fireplace at the old JMS Gun Club in Delaware, Ohio on a cold winter weekend. I had a great time traveling to and competing in the State of Ohio Trap Championships and the Grand American for more than a dozen years in Vandalia, Ohio. Visiting several sporting clays courses in the Midwest for weekend shoots (and just good times) with our little shooting club, "Shoot 'Em All," will remain in my memory bank forever.

I dedicate this book to fellow shooting friends, instructors, teachers and "buddies." Taking shooting lessons from great all-American trap shooters Frank Little, Kay Ohye and Phil Kiner was a tremendous help in improving my shooting ability.

Sporting clay instructor Jim Arnold had the patience to stand behind me and see thousands of misses and thousands of hits until I got it right. Jim was my teacher when I earned a level one National Sporting Clays Association shooting instruction certificate.

The Orvis Shooting School was all about the Churchill's Move, Mount and Shoot style. The USA Shooting Program at the Olympic Training Center in Colorado Springs for coaching shotgun shooting sports is a fabulous week. It is hard to describe the wonderful young shooters who represent our country in shotgun shooting sports around the world.

John Ransom, who shot with me in my first attempt at Amateur Trapshooting Association registered targets, was kind enough to endure watching me fix my pump shotgun after nearly every other shot. John continued to teach me more about trapshooting than I can ever remember or repay.

This book is also dedicated to good friends and shooters Bill Weaver and Mike Galbreath, with whom I traveled around Ohio for the zone shoots, the State of Ohio Championships, the Grand American and many JMS Shooting Club shoots. It was always a lot of fun to play a few tricks on them, and we were guaranteed to share a good laugh.

This is dedicated also to Jim Hintz, John Streit and John Jankowski. I shot skeet with them regularly on Wednesday nights and won or lost more single malt scotch drinks than one should be allowed. The steak dinners and hours of conversation and arguing about shotguns and shooting can never be replaced.

In Arizona, I dedicate this to Al Suter, my weekly buddy for breakfast at The Good Egg and shooting sporting clays with a little bet on the side. This is to Rick Smith, who never misses in skeet, and who watches and laughs as I always miss low six. We both enjoy the new Olympic Trap field at Ben Avery in Phoenix, Arizona, and it is currently our greatest challenge in shotgun shooting sports.

I have been blessed and fortunate to have so many wonderful shooting experiences while developing lifelong friends. My hope is that many of the lessons I have learned from these friends, instructors and by trial and error will be communicated in this book—helping you shoot a little better and enjoy the shotgun shooting sports at another level.

PULL!

Mike McGuire

AUTHOR MIKE McGUIRE'S SHOTGUNNING BIO

Like thousands of other young boys, I was very fortunate to be introduced to the wonderful sport of shotgun shooting by my father. I spent my early years shooting a .22-caliber rifle and my Red Ryder BB Gun at bottles (and squirrels) before I could "go along" and watch my dad hunt upland birds. Finally, one day when I was about 10 years old, I shot his Ithaca 12-gauge shotgun for the first time, and I was hooked. By the age of 16, I was reloading shells and shooting trap at the old Winchester Gun Club in Columbus, Ohio. I was a member of the single trap house Dublin Gun Club in Dublin, Ohio, which later became the site of Wendy's restaurants' headquarters.

After high school, off I went to The Ohio State University and to Vietnam, and I got married and had kids. My shotgun shooting ceased until I was in my early 30s. At a Fourth of July picnic, I heard about the JMS Gun Club (now Black Wing Shooting Center) in Delaware, Ohio; more importantly, I heard about Jaqua's Fine Guns (a candy store for shotgun enthusiasts) in Findlay, Ohio. My interest in shotgun shooting was piqued once again! The following week, I went to JMS to check it out, bought a new Browning Citori Plus shotgun at Jaqua's, became a lifetime member of the Amateur Trapshooting Association and shot my first registered targets.

Fast forward. I now have been shooting clay targets for more than 30 years. I have shot all over the United States and some in Europe and South America. Now that I am in the third quarter of my life, my enjoyment of shotgun shooting sports continues to grow every year. I'll shoot any game that anybody wants to shoot—on any given day!

INTRODUCTION

Shotguns and Clay Target Sports TRIVIA Q + A is my seventh in a series of trivia books, and it's one of my most enjoyable projects. I wanted the book to capture some of the great history and traditions of shotgun shooting. At the same time, I wanted it to be informative about shotguns: what and how things happen when shooting. The clay target shotgun shooting sports are covered in a way that I hope will be a good teaching tool. I want readers to have a newfound understanding and respect for shotguns, shooting, and the clay target shooting sports. Shotgun questions are asked throughout the book, but the first 800 questions cover the trap and skeet games. The last 200 questions cover sporting clays, FITASC, ZZ Birds and 5-Stand, among others. For some questions, nobody will know the answer, but that is part of what makes trivia fun.

Many of the questions and answers were taken right off the top of my head because I have been lucky to spend so many years shooting. I used the Internet, along with the rule books, to verify and double-check many of the questions and answers. I read extensively from my shotgun book collection of more than 500 books looking for the unique, different and somewhat difficult questions. I can only say a very sincere "thank you" to the many authors, instructors and friends who have shared their knowledge and interest in advancing shotgunning and the clay target shooting sports. The best part is…I still learn something every time I go shooting!

HOW TO USE
SHOTGUNS + CLAY TARGET SPORTS TRIVIA Q + A

My trivia questions are meant to be fun, thought provoking, educational, somewhat confusing and tricky. But best of all, they are meant to bring back good memories while testing your knowledge of a particular subject. *Shotguns + Clay Target Sports TRIVIA Q + A* is no different. I offer the following suggestions on how to use this trivia for your greater enjoyment.

The book is laid out in a format of 20 questions and 20 answers, so shotgun enthusiasts can go along at their own pace. Each correct answer could be worth five points within a group of questions, and individuals or teams could be awarded prizes for their skill and knowledge of shotguns and shotgun shooting sports trivia.

Pre-Event Parties... This is a fun way to meet new shooters, sponsors, guests, officials and others before the shooting starts.

Vendors Booths... Pass time before or after you shoot with some of your favorite vendors and suppliers while visiting their booth. Some will probably like to use questions in their business.

On the Road... While driving to and from the shooting championships, trivia can help make the miles pass faster. Play to see who drives and who asks the questions, or play for who buys the next tank of gas, food, snacks or cocktails. Or play for a few American Yankee Dollars.

On an Airplane, Bus or Train... This is a very good way to study and improve your knowledge of shotgun shooting championships, history, traditions, shotguns, famous shooters, shotgun manufacturers, records and a whole lot more. Upon your arrival, impress your friends with your expanded shotgun and shotgun shooting knowledge.

Club House Grill Room...A pizza or a hamburger and fries, along with a cold beer, always tastes better with great shotgun shooting sports trivia Q + A, conversations, discussions and arguments. And it doesn't get any better than with your shooting buddies.

In Your Gun Bag... You should have a copy of the book in your gun bag to have with you in case of a long rain delay or other occurrences while either on the course or inside the clubhouse. It will help pass the time and create some fun and laughs.

In the Bathroom...OK, but please keep the book on your nightstand or bookshelf.

Please send me the unique ways you have used *Shotguns + Clay Target Sports TRIVIA Q + A* to enhance your respect and love for shotguns and the shotgun shooting sports.

Aim high, and shoot straight!

Mike McGuire
Author & Ole Trapshooter

TABLE OF CONTENTS

Questions group 1

1-1   What is the most popular shotgun in history?

1-2   What is the ATA Singles long-run record?

1-3   Who wrote the first rule book and what was the first trapshooting association?

1-4   Who shot the first ATA Grand Slam (200 Singles, 100 27-yard Handicap and 100 straight Doubles)?

1-5   Which has a longer barrel—a shotgun or a rifle?

1-6   **T or F** The amount of choke is determined by subtracting the inside diameter of the choked area from the bore diameter.

1-7   What are the most popular and common, and the largest and smallest gauges in shotguns?

1-8   What is a "Dutched Pair?"

1-9   If the stock on your shotgun is too short, where will it shoot?

1-10   List the six parts that make up a modern plastic shotgun shell.

1-11   **T or F** U.S. and European bore diameters are identical.

1-12   What two accessory pieces of safety equipment are mandatory to shoot trap or skeet and all other clay target sports?

1-13   Where does a shot string start?

1-14   What does the speed of the "spinning revolutions" have to do with the ease of breaking a bird?

1-15   **T or F** Skilled trapshooters used Model 97 Winchester shotguns to deflect hand grenades during WWI.

1-16   American gun designer John Browning is credited with how many patents?

1-17   Which 12-month period makes up a target year for the ATA?

1-18   What are the projectiles called that come from a shotgun?

1-19   What distance in yardage is American Doubles Trap shot?

1-20   **T or F** The "Drop of the Comb" (between 1-5/8″ and 2-1/2″) will prove to fit the majority of shooters.

Answers group 1

1-1   Remington Model 870, introduced in 1950, over 10 million manufactured since.

1-2   2,166 shot by David Shaeffer, Jr. on August 20, 2009 at Cardinal Center in Marengo, Ohio

1-3   The American Shooting Association, 1889

1-4   Dan Orlich, 1964

1-5   Shotguns, unless modified for some reason or design.

1-6   True, good math formula to remember.

1-7   10 gauge (largest); 410 (smallest), 6 popular gauges in all: 10, 12, 16, 20, 28 and 410

1-8   This occurs when both targets are missed in doubles.

1-9   High. If the stock is too long, it will shoot low.

1-10 Plastic shell case, brass head, primer, gunpowder, wad and shot. People add in "crimp" for #7.

1-11 False. Generally speaking the answer is NO. Europeans are .005 less than U.S. dimensional standards.

1-12 Eye and ear protection—NO exceptions! Never shoot without wearing both of them!

1-13 At the muzzle, as the shot starts to spread and string out as it leaves the barrel.

1-14 The faster it spins, the easier it is to break!

1-15 True! How times have changed.

1-16 128 gun patents!

1-17 November 1st through October 31st

1-18 Shot or pellets and sometimes load

1-19 16 yards, same distance as singles

1-20 True! 90% of the shooters

Questions group 2

2-1   Who is the largest firearms manufacturer in the USA?

2-2   **T or F** A rifled barrel is unsuitable for firing shot, but necessary for a slug round.

2-3   Does "high-brass" vs. "low-brass" mean anything other than possible trademarks?

2-4   Name the two types of fixed action shotguns.

2-5   Where is the most comprehensive collection of firearms in the world?

2-6   What is the first thing you should do with your NEW trap shotgun?

2-7   In what gauge(s) was the Browning Automatic 5 (Auto 5 or A-5) available when introduced?

2-8   A new lady trapshooter will be assigned what handicap yardage?

2-9   Olympic trap targets are thrown at what speed?

2-10   **T or F** Does the ATA (trapshooting) and NSSA (skeet) use the same size standard clay target in their American championships?

2-11   What three factors affect air density?

2-12   When moving to post one in trap from post five, what should you do for the squad leader?

2-13   Who invented skeet shooting?

2-14   What is "porting?"

2-15   What year did Winchester start to sell smokeless shotgun shells?

2-16   **T or F** The first Grand Americans with live birds were shot for ten years from 1893 to 1902.

2-17   At what handicap distance should a trapshooter go from #8s to #7-1/2s, if they like #8s for 16-yard singles?

2-18   **T or F** Shooting a double-trigger shotgun takes time and is a learned skill.

2-19   How are the following different? Invector-plus, Mobilchoke, Rem-choke and Win-choke

2-20   How far apart should your feet be in a trapshooting stance?

Answers group 2

2-1   Remington Arms Company

2-2   True

2-3   Yes, "high-brass" is normally a higher-powered shell than "low-brass."

2-4   Semi-automatic and pump

2-5   The Cody Firearms Museum, Cody, Wyoming

2-6   Pattern it! Find the "Point of Impact" (POI)

2-7   Three gauges, 12, 16 and 20

2-8   19 yards

2-9   Between 61 and 65 mph

2-10   True, 108mm

2-11   Temperature, humidity and air pressure

2-12   Nod your head that you are ready to shoot.

2-13   Charles E. Davis, 1915, from Andover, Massachusetts

2-14   The addition of small holes near the end of the shotgun's barrel.

2-15   1903–1960, Remington introduced plastic hull shotgun shells

2-16   True

2-17   20 yards, #7-1/2s work better all the way back to the 27-yard line (back fence)

2-18   True, but they are fun shotguns to shoot.

2-19   All of the chokes have a different thread pattern for their screw-in choke systems.

2-20   Varies among shooters, but all should provide a stable center of gravity…armpit wide or shoulder width, a casual stance, heels 8 inches apart, similar to when you are talking with friends.

Questions   group 3

3-1   What are the three most common metals used in shot?

3-2   From numerous studies, what is the minimum number of pellets needed to hit a clay target to break it and register a "dead bird?"

3-3   How much load (shot string) spreads out during flight, is called what?

3-4   Name the two types of break-action breech-loading double shotguns.

3-5   Name the five major parts or areas of a shotgun wood stock.

3-6   **T or F** The larger the diameter of your shot string, the smaller your pointing error can be and still hit the target.

3-7   When two contestants fire at the same target in trap, how is it scored?

3-8   What is the cardinal rule for safe shotgun shooting?

3-9   **T or F** A scorekeeper announces the results of every shot in doubles, but not necessarily in singles or handicap.

3-10   Who developed the over and under (O/U) shotgun patent in 1913?

3-11   "Best gun" is a shotgun term to describe what?

3-12   What was the inscription on Holland & Holland shotguns before 1876?

3-13   Approximately how long can a lead shot string be (including deformed flyers)?

3-14   Are different chokes used for trapshooting and skeet shooting?

3-15   A straight grip is often called by what other name?

3-16   What is a shell in which the primer fails to fire when struck by the firing pin?

3-17   **T or F** A beavertail fore-end is wider than a normal fore-end.

3-18   What bad habit does a built-in interrupter on an oscillating trap prevent?

3-19   What is the radius, in degrees, that American Trap targets are thrown between posts?

3-20   **T or F** A trigger block safety is not automatically engaged when the hammers are cocked.

Answers group 3

3-1	Lead, steel and bismuth
3-2	Three
3-3	The pattern, which is a two-dimensional representation of the shot string at a given distance.
3-4	Side-by-side and the over and under (O/U)
3-5	The grip, the comb, heel, butt and toe
3-6	False. It's a greater point error, rather than smaller.
3-7	NO target!
3-8	DO NOT depend on the "safety," it is a mechanical device and it could malfunction. This is true for all types of guns.
3-9	True! "Dead Pair", "Lost, Dead", "Dead, Lost" or "Lost a Pair"
3-10	Woodward, a London, England gun maker
3-11	The highest quality double-barrel shotguns.
3-12	H. Holland for Harris Holland, founder 1835
3-13	10-12 feet long at its effective range. It changes from the muzzle until it hits the ground.
3-14	Yes, but each shooter should determine which choke(s) work best by shooting and using pattern boards.
3-15	English grip
3-16	Misfire
3-17	True
3-18	"Reading the Trap" or guessing the flight of the next clay pigeon.
3-19	34 degrees between each post (left and right)
3-20	False. A design developed in 1882 by Anson & Deeley and still prevalent in modern box-lock actions.

Questions group 4

4-1   **T or F** In regard to shot size, the larger the number, the smaller the diameter of the shot pellet.

4-2   What distance is recommended to pattern your trap and skeet shotguns?

4-3   What is the most effective shot size for 12-gauge trapshooters?

4-4   What type of wad would you use to open up your pattern once the shot has left the muzzle?

4-5   How many targets make up the "All-Around" Championship at major trapshooting tournaments?

4-6   By many (most) shotgun experts, what is the most important invention of all time for shotguns?

4-7   Which length of a shotgun barrel is easier to point, a short one or a long one?

4-8   Who invented the choke bore shotgun?

4-9   _____ _____ is the hinged front trigger that allows it to move forward when the rear trigger is used on a double trigger shotgun.

4-10   What was the first electric trap to have a built-in electric release?

4-11   Name the four best London gun makers in 1900.

4-12   **T or F** The original skeet course was a 25-yard radius circle with the trap at 12 o'clock.

4-13   What was the name of the famous choke system developed by Winchester?

4-14   _____ _____ is the yardage assigned to trapshooters who have not met the minimum target requirement.

4-15   Which fore-end is carved to resemble the beak of a bird?

4-16   _____ is the moving part that allows you to load, fire and unload your shotgun.

4-17   Which gauge was/is called "The All Gauge?"

4-18   Which shotgun design, box-lock or side-lock provides more space for an engraver's artwork?

4-19   What is the title of the shot gunners' annual guide book used for nearly 20 years?

4-20   Name the major shotgun manufacturing cities in the United Kingdom, Italy, Germany and Spain.

Answers group 4

4-1   True

4-2   40 yards for trap, 25 yards for skeet

4-3   #7-1/2, but many will argue #8. Better yet, study the performance figures!

4-4   "Spreader Wad" but not allowed in competitions

4-5   400 targets: 200 Singles, 100 Doubles and 100 Handicap

4-6   Choke bore, author states many will argue for the plastic wad introduced in 1965.

4-7   The longer barrel

4-8   Fred Kimble, 1868, Trapshooting Hall of Fame member

4-9   Articulated Trigger

4-10   Western white flyer electric trap (V1524A)

4-11   Purdey & Sons, Boss & Co., Holland and Holland and Woodward—names a shotgun enthusiast should know.

4-12   True, called "Clock Shooting"

4-13   Winchoke

4-14   Penalty yardage

4-15   Schnabel fore-end (Shnobel or Schnobel)

4-16   Action

4-17   12 gauge—most popular shotgun shooting gauge

4-18   Side-lock

4-19   *Black's Wing & Clay Water Fowl*

4-20   Birmingham, England; Valtrompia, Italy; Suhl, Germany; and Elbar, Spain

Questions group 5

5-1   What did George Ligowsky invent?

5-2   How many trap targets of the same kind, shot in one day, make up a "Marathon?"

5-3   What was the title of the first shotgun trapshooting publication (magazine) circa 1880?

5-4   **T or F** Steel shot is less dense than lead, so it loses its speed fastener in the air.

5-5   What is the choke restriction on a full choke?

5-6   What is the primary purpose of the plastic wad in the shotgun shell?

5-7   What does "nose over toes" refer to in your shooting stance?

5-8   What determines the speed at which a clay target leaves the trap?

5-9   **T or F** It is best to choose shooting glasses with interchangeable colored lenses.

5-10   Where is the recommended "hold point" for post three on the trap house for 16-yard singles?

5-11   What is the max velocity for trap loads: 1-1/8 oz., 1 oz. and 7/8 oz.?

5-12   What year was the ATA Hall of Fame established?

5-13   Name the four special measurements that are very important on any shotgun stock for proper fit.

5-14   If your "gunning buddy" is talking about "twisted" barrels, what is he most likely referring to?

5-15   Which type of trigger is commonly suggested to use to help with flinching?

5-16   **T or F** The four major disciplines in skeet are American, English, International and Doubles.

5-17   Of what two materials are clay targets manufactured?

5-18   What type of triggers are most over and under (O/U) shotguns manufactured with today?

5-19   Who won fifteen gold medals individually or as a team member, in skeet, from 1979 to 1992?

5-20   With your muzzle elevated to 30 degrees, which shot, #7-1/2 or #8, travels farthest?

Answers group 5

5-1   The clay pigeon, 1880

5-2   500 or 1,000 targets

5-3   Smokeless Shot

5-4   True

5-5   .035 inches smaller than the bore

5-6   The plastic wad provides a gas seal, which propels the shot down the barrel.

5-7   A slight bend at the waist

5-8   The tension placed on the spring that moves (releases) the throwing arm holding the clay pigeon.

5-9   True. Light conditions change often and you have to adapt.

5-10 Slightly right (right-hand shooter) of center, front edge of the trap house or higher (your personal adjustment). If ON dead center you might lose sight of the bird (blur) under your barrel.

5-11 1-1/8 oz. (1290 fps), 1 oz. (1325 fps) and 7/8 oz. (1350 fps)

5-12 1968 established, first induction of 15 ATA Hall of Famers, August 19, 1969

5-13 Length of pull, drop at the comb, drop at the heel and cast (on or off)

5-14 Damascus "Twist" barrels made before the 1900s

5-15 Release trigger. Be extra careful when learning to shoot release triggers!

5-16 True

5-17 Coal tar (pitch) 20-40% and pulverized limestone rock (filler material)

5-18 Inertia triggers—the first shot recoil enables the trigger to re-set and shoot the second shot.

5-19 USA Shooting (Hall of Fame) member Matthew Dryke, Olympic Gold in 1984, two World Championships 1983 & 1986, Pan Am Games 1983 & 1987

5-20 #7-1/2 goes a little over 200 yards, #8 goes a little less than 200 yards—a safety zone is considered 300 yards

Questions group 6

6-1   List the eight most common chokes in order, from open to tight.

6-2   **T or F** One of the biggest mistakes a trap or a shot gunner makes is not "patterning his gun."

6-3   Name the three types of ribs on side-by-side shotgun barrels.

6-4   Skeet shooters like what type of fore-end for a smooth and quick swing?

6-5   Did the Browning Auto-5 and Remington Model 11 both have a "square back" receiver?

6-6   Which gauge shotgun typically weighs less than a 12-gauge, shoots like a 20-gauge, and is one that you can carry and shoot all day in the field?

6-7   The initials "DT" are an abbreviation on Beretta shotguns for what reason?

6-8   When and where was the first National Skeet Championship held?

6-9   What are the following: "Star," "Lark," "Best," "Keystone," "Clipper" and "Universal?"

6-10 If you find a consistent hole when you pattern your shotgun, what should you do to correct the problem?

6-11 **T or F** In trap, if a shooter fires at a "slow pull" (not required to shoot at), the result is not scored.

6-12 A shotgun stock, that is longer and has less drop than standard, is called what type of stock?

6-13 **T or F** These four factors are required to have a successful trap shot: a correct horizontal and vertical lead, a continuous moving swing and follow-through.

6-14 What determines the grade of walnut gun stocks?

6-15 What does a big "R" (in red or fluorescent colors) mean on a gun stock or pistol grip?

6-16 How much "choke" does a cylinder bore have?

6-17 **T or F** The rules allow one to shoot a 28-gauge shotgun in a 20-gauge skeet event.

6-18 What happens if the grip on the shotgun is too thin?

6-19 When shooting skeet doubles, which shot is always shot first, the outgoing or incoming?

6-20 If you are in a shooting slump, what should be the first thing you check?

Answers group 6

6-1   Cylinder (bore), skeet, improved cylinder, light modified, modified, improved modified, light full and full

6-2   True! Why wouldn't you want to know how your shotgun performs!

6-3   Concave Rib, Churchill and Flat Rib

6-4   Beavertail

6-5   Yes. Both the Browning Auto-5 and the Remington Model 11 were identical shotguns.

6-6   16-gauge. See the 16-Gauge Society at www.16ga.com.

6-7   "Detachable Triggers"

6-8   1935 in Cleveland, Ohio

6-9   Early clay pigeon names from a large list of manufacturers

6-10   Try cleaning the bore (barrel) to remove plastic fouling, or (if clean) try a different choke manufacturer.

6-11   False. The shot result is scored as dead or lost.

6-12   Trap stock

6-13   True! A stopped shotgun will miss every time!

6-14   Type of features or fancy grain in the wood and wood pattern symmetry.

6-15   This shotgun has a Release Trigger!

6-16   None. NO constriction in the barrel at any point.

6-17   True. In skeet you can always shoot a smaller gauge than the gauge of the event

6-18   Shooter will dip his elbow on the grip hand, which pulls the barrel in that direction.

6-19   The outgoing target is always shot first!

6-20   The position of your eyes when your shotgun is mounted.

Questions group 7

7-1   When did America win its first gold medal in Olympic Trap?

7-2   What famous shotgun book did Captain A.H. Bogardus write?

7-3   A shotgun is known by what other names?

7-4   Who invented the first semi-automatic shotgun and the lever-action repeating shotgun?

7-5   What year was the first official ATA average book published?

7-6   With a proper set-up (stance), how many degrees of a controlled swing (rotation) are you afforded to move?

7-7   What is the official magazine of the Amateur Trapshooting Association (ATA)?

7-8   What are the two most popular 12-gauge shot sizes and chokes for American Trap singles?

7-9   What is the most popular shot size and choke for American skeet?

7-10   What was the Sargeant System?

7-11   Which type(s) of shotgun(s) have a barrel screw cap?

7-12   Who manufactures the "Made in America" 12-gauge Phoenix shotgun?

7-13   **T or F** When reloading mixed hulls from different manufacturers, it is OK as long as they are all the same gauge.

7-14   The 3/4-style clay target (New York style) is also known by what name?

7-15   **T or F** Longer length barrels make the pellets move faster and go farther.

7-16   What is the portion of the stock on which a trapshooter places his cheek?

7-17   Besides American and Olympic Trap disciplines, name three other popular trap games.

7-18   What color should the underside of your hat brim be to help with eye strain?

7-19   **T or F** A stock that is too long will cause more kick to the shoulder than one that is too short.

7-20   **T or F** A back-bored barrel promotes less deformed shot, thus better patterning and a shorter shot string.

Answers group 7

7-1   1912 Olympic games in Stockholm, Sweden; won by Jay Graham

7-2   *Field, Cover and Trapshooting,* 1899

7-3   Scattergun or peppergun

7-4   John Browning

7-5   1914, now considered "The Bible" for ATA Trapshooters

7-6   180 degrees of swing (rotation)

7-7   *Trap & Field,* 317-633-8800

7-8   #7-1/2 and #8 shot; full or modified chokes

7-9   #9 with a skeet choke

7-10   1885, three traps, four feet apart, targets thrown from unknown trap at unknown angle

7-11   Semi-automatics and pump shotguns

7-12   Ithaca Shotguns of Upper Sandusky, Ohio

7-13   False. NEVER mix components when reloading! A major safety rule!

7-14   "DOP" target, it's all about the paint scheme.

7-15   False

7-16   The comb

7-17   Universal Trench, Automatic Ball Trap (ABT) and Wobble/Continental

7-18   Select a dark color that will not reflect off the concrete pad. I personally like a dark green or blue.

7-19   False. A stock too short will kick more.

7-20   True

Questions   group 8

8-1   **T or F**   A "dusted target" is scored as a hit ("dead bird").

8-2   Which shot pellet deforms more, lead or steel?

8-3   When shooting a clay target, what two types of vision come into play?

8-4   Who invented the "shot tower" to manufacture spherical lead shot?

8-5   What yardage do men start at when shooting handicap targets?

8-6   A .410 bore shotgun is actually what gauge?

8-7   Clay target throwers (traps) are available in what two basic categories?

8-8   **T or F**   One trap theory is that on posts #1 and #2 you shoot the left side of the target, post #3 straightaway, and posts #4 and #5 you shoot the right side of the target.

8-9   **T or F**   When shooting trap doubles, you are only allowed to shoot at each target once.

8-10   Who produced the standards for screw threads used on shotguns that still exist today (after one hundred years)?

8-11   What is William Harden Foster known for in skeet shooting?

8-12   Where, in a barrel, is lead shot deformed upon firing the shotgun?

8-13   Who broke the first 100 x 100 doubles at the Grand American?

8-14   What is considered by many as the ideal trigger-pull weight on a single trigger clay target shooting shotgun?

8-15   **T or F**   In trap, a "high gun" refers to the shooters gun position on his shoulder.

8-16   **T or F**   The length of the shell designated on the shotgun barrel is after the shell is fired.

8-17   What two types of adjustable triggers are usually offered for shotguns?

8-18   List the four shot load weight limits for the four gauges in American skeet.

8-19   On the score sheet, what does an "O" and an "X" designate?

8-20   What is the mechanical device used to eject empty shells from the chamber(s)?

Answers group 8

8-1   False. NOT a hit or DEAD bird. A visible piece must leave the clay target, not just "dust."

8-2   Lead

8-3   Primary vision (clay target), peripheral Vision (everything else)

8-4   William Watts, patented in 1783, Bristol, United Kingdom

8-5   20-yard line, longest earned yardage is 27 yards

8-6   67-gauge

8-7   Manual and automatic

8-8   True! But author thinks this is a good question to discuss with other trap shooters.

8-9   True. One shot per target.

8-10   John Robertson, famous British gun maker for Boss & Co.

8-11   In 1923 he cut the circle course (Clock Course) into a (1/2) semi-circle with two traps houses, one low and one high.

8-12   At ignition, forcing cone and choke

8-13   Rudy Etchen, 1950

8-14   3-1/2 to 4 pounds of pull, but it is a personal choice

8-15   False. "High gun" is the gun position above the trap house before calling for the bird.

8-16   True, remember the shell is crimped and opens when fired.

8-17   Notched (preset increments) or variable (you set it...a more accurate fit)

8-18   12-gauge (1-1/8 oz.), 20 gauge (7/8 oz.), 28 gauge (3/4 oz.) and 410 gauge (1/2 oz.)

8-19   "O" for Lost Targets and "X" for Dead Targets

8-20   Ejector

Questions group 9

9-1 **T or F** The tighter the choke, the more lead shot will be deformed (dented), causing more uneven patterns.

9-2 Name the three types of actions in a break action shotgun.

9-3 **T or F** Circa 1920 there were an estimated 4,000-plus trap clubs in America with over half a million members.

9-4 **T or F** The more choke you have the longer the distance for a more effective range of shot.

9-5 Who originated "glass ball" shooting in America to substitute for shooting live birds?

9-6 How many set programs for the fifteen traps in Olympic Trap are there, that are used around the world?

9-7 What does "Pigeon Grade" refer to on a shotgun?

9-8 In which Olympics was International Skeet shot for the first time?

9-9 What is a shot string?

9-10 Where is the safety located on an over and under (O/U) shotgun?

9-11 **T or F** When you hear the bird released before you see it, you should shoulder your shotgun immediately, locate the bird and swing your shotgun in the correct direction.

9-12 When are "flash targets" used?

9-13 Which actions use concealed, self-locking hammers in a break-open action?

9-14 **T or F** The sun can be considered interference in trap and a "no bird" called for a lost bird.

9-15 **T or F** Plastic wads reduce pattern consistency by leaving plastic fouling in the shotgun barrel.

9-16 What city claims to be the birthplace and early home to trapshooting in the United States?

9-17 **T or F** Maintaining an upright body position and with good pivoting, a shot gunner will improve his gun mounting skills.

9-18 Which hand on the shotgun is responsible for vertical and horizontal movement of the shotgun?

9-19 What should be your weight distribution in your stance when shotgun shooting?

9-20 What does the term "anticipation" mean in shotgun shooting?

Answers group 9

9-1   True

9-2   The side-lock, the box-lock and the trigger plate

9-3   True! Trap was called "Sport Alluring."

9-4   True

9-5   Charles Portlock of Boston, 1866; 1st competition 1867

9-6   Nine programs

9-7   Wood quality on stock and forearm

9-8   1968, at the Mexico Summer Olympics in Mexico City, Mexico

9-9   The length of the shot column from the first pellet to the last one out of the barrel.

9-10   On top of the action by the release

9-11   False. See the bird first, then shoulder your shotgun.

9-12   For final events in International competitions and televised events. Common in the Olympics.

9-13   Box-lock and side-lock

9-14   False. The sun is not considered in scoring trap shots.

9-15   True! The reason you might have holes in your patterns and need to clean your shotgun and chokes.

9-16   Cincinnati, Ohio, The Queen City, 1831

9-17   True! Plus practice, practice, practice!

9-18   Left hand (right-hand shooter) when in proper position; the forward hand

9-19   Approximately 60-40 or 65-35 with the weight on the ball of the leading foot (leg). Remember, be comfortable.

9-20   Stopping the gun movement upon firing the shot. You will shoot behind (missing) the bird!

Questions group 10

10-1 What was used for birds during the first contested trapshooting contests?

10-2 What type of shotgun was commonly called a "fowling piece" for shooting live birds?

10-3 **T or F** One of the purposes of the rib on the barrel is to dissipate heat and prevent the "mirage effect."

10-4 What diameter-size circle is usually used for patterning a shotgun?

10-5 What is the largest amount (by weight) of shot you can use in trapshooting?

10-6 **T or F** A second shot may be used for each clay target without a penalty in Olympic Trap.

10-7 At approximately what yardage are targets broken in American Singles Trap?

10-8 **T or F** The average trap and skeet squad is composed of five shooters; six in Olympic Trap.

10-9 What is Juglans Negra?

10-10 What is a "mental interruption?"

10-11 With a low gun position in International Skeet, what factor is important in regard to your stance?

10-12 **T or F** A shot gunner with too wide of a stance will restrict his upper body movement because he is less balanced, restricting his range of swing.

10-13 Which shotgun manufacturer uses the Graco "CTS" adjustable comb system?

10-14 In what countries are the following fine shotgun manufacturers located: F.lli Piotti, Zoli, F.lli Rizzini, A & S Famars

10-15 Which powder burns quicker, a shotgun (shot shell) powder or a rifle (bullet) powder?

10-16 Where is the "forcing cone" located in a shotgun barrel?

10-17 If a 3″, 12-gauge shell fits into a shotgun chamber marked 2-3/4″, is it safe to shoot this shell?

10-18 **T or F** One of the best things about shotgun shooting is that sound fundamental shooters can be cloned.

10-19 What is the maximum target angle in Olympic Trap?

10-20 **T or F** Eastern United States trap birds fly the same as Western U.S. trap birds.

Answers group 10

10-1   Passenger pigeons

10-2   Side-by-side

10-3   True. A ventilated rib.

10-4   30" diameter circle, patterning is usually shot at 40 yards for trap; 25 yards for skeet

10-5   1-1/8 ounce of shot in a 12-gauge shotgun

10-6   True. You have two shots to break the bird.

10-7   32 to 41 yards, depends on the shooters skill level

10-8   True. Trap is always five or less, skeet is best with five or less, and six for Olympic Trap.

10-9   Walnut, commonly called Eastern black walnut, American walnut, Black walnut or California black—most popular woods used for gunstocks

10-10   Anything that changes or interrupts your shooting rhythm. Start all over or you will probably miss the bird.

10-11   A consistently smooth gun mount every time!

10-12   True. Remember, a comfortable stance.

10-13   SKB Shotguns

10-14   Italy

10-15   Shotgun powder—reason for the thick-walled breech

10-16   Right in front of the chamber

10-17   Absolutely NOT! Never safe! Know your shot shells and your gun!

10-18   False. All shotgun shooters are individuals with a "personal style."

10-19   45 degrees

10-20   False! Eastern targets are thrown a little faster because of the humidity and the Western birds are a "little bouncy" because of the higher altitudes.

Questions · group 11

11-1　What is the minimum distance a singles trap target should be thrown?

11-2　The shooter moves the foregrip backward to eject the spent hull through the port and then moves the foregrip forward to load a live shell into the chamber. Name the shotgun.

11-3　**T or F**　With an over and under (O/U) shotgun you need to only pattern the top barrel.

11-4　What year were women allowed to shoot the Grand American Handicap?

11-5　Many factors determine proper gun fit, but which one is arguably the most important?

11-6　Name the two types or variety that screw-in chokes come in.

11-7　Which shotgun manufacturer patented the single trigger for double guns?

11-8　**T or F**　The choke causes the center mass pellets of the shot column to accelerate.

11-9　A regular skeet target must pass through a 3-foot diameter hoop. How many feet above the ground is that at the target crossing point?

11-10　What is the first indication you have an adjustable trigger on your target shotgun?

11-11　**T or F**　ATA rules allow for changing the height of the bird due to weather conditions or wind.

11-12　How long does a trap or skeet shooter take when it is his turn to shoot?

11-13　In Olympic Trap, how fast do shooters shoot straightaway and angle shots?

11-14　**T or F**　Olympic Trap, International Trap and Bunker Trap are all one and the same.

11-15　Name the three types of target lead referred to in shotgun shooting.

11-16　What are the two types of membership in the Amateur Trapshooting Association (ATA)?

11-17　**T or F**　Most trap shotguns with a "full choke" will place 70% of the shot pattern in a 30″ circle at 40 yards.

11-18　What is the only shotgun shell gauge with a mandated color for safety concerns?

11-19　What is the Bleimeister Process?

11-20　What organization sets the standards for international targets?

Answers group 11

11-1 Flying not less than 49 yards, nor more than 51 yards

11-2 Pump shotgun

11-3 False. Pattern both barrels to make sure they pattern "real close" (the same) to each other.

11-4 December 1915

11-5 Length of the gun stock

11-6 Flush mounted and extended

11-7 Boss & Co.

11-8 True

11-9 15 feet high, and fly from 55 to 65 yards in still air measured from the skeet houses.

11-10 A small socket head (Allen head) set screw. Your shotgun should come with the proper hex key (Allen wrench) to make adjustments.

11-11 True. 2-foot variation of (8 to 10 feet) at ten feet in front of the trap house.

11-12 Maybe five seconds for the whole process, but about 1.2 seconds from calling for the bird(s) until you dismount. It takes about 2/10s of a second to determine to fire, pull the trigger and hit the firing pin.

11-13 Straightaway .5 to .6/10s of a second; angles .6 to .8/10s of a second, second shots follow at .3 to .4/10s of a second later.

11-14 True. Just different names from different organizations and countries.

11-15 Swing-through, pull-away and sustained (maintain) lead. Learn all three and understand how they work and shoot them in practice.

11-16 Annual and Life. I suggest a Life Membership if at all affordable in your shooting budget.

11-17 True. This is a good goal to have when patterning your full choke for trapshooting.

11-18 20-gauge—yellow! A safety issue so you don't put the wrong shell in a 16- or 12-gauge chamber

11-19 A method to manufacture lead shot; has replaced the shot tower.

11-20 UIT/ISSF—Now the ISSF International Shooting Sports Federation

Questions group 12

12-1   Guessing the angle of the clay target flight before one calls "pull" for the bird is called what?

12-2   Who is the world's largest manufacturer of pump action shotguns?

12-3   Who invented the first practical glass ball trap in 1877?

12-4   **T or F** The shooter or scorekeeper must see a visible piece or chip to declare a bird "dead" on a legally thrown target.

12-5   Who is known as "The Royal" gun maker?

12-6   **T or F** The trigger pull on a skeet shotgun should be set with a drag of 3-1/2 to 4 lbs.

12-7   How far is a bunker (Olympic or International) trap target set to fly?

12-8   Which English shotgun manufacturer is famous for their "Rose and Scroll" engraving pattern?

12-9   **T or F** The Purdy single trigger works both by inertia and mechanically; therefore the firing sequence is fixed and barrel selection is not possible.

12-10   What features do interchangeable spacers affect on a shotgun stock?

12-11   What is a blank?

12-12   **T or F** An easy solution to solving an inertia trigger problem of not firing the second shot might be to change barrel selection.

12-13   In which clay shooting game does the clay pigeon have a reinforcing ring on the throwing ring?

12-14   In a trap competition with six classes, what percentage is required to be a Triple A shooter?

12-15   **T or F** Porting your shotgun barrels reduces recoil.

12-16   What size (diameter) were the first glass balls?

12-17   **T or F** There is a 0-to-3 second delay in releasing the bird after the shooter calls "pull" in International Skeet.

12-18   When the trap is set to oscillate up and down, as well as side-to-side, one thinks of what type of trap game?

12-19   "Shell catchers" are used on what type of shotguns?

12-20   Thomas Boss worked for what two famous gun makers before starting Boss & Co. in 1812?

Answers group 12

12-1   "Reading the Trap"

12-2   Mossberg

12-3   Capt. A.H. Bogardus, ball flew 28 to 35 yards in a long arc

12-4   True

12-5   Holland & Holland, 1885

12-6   False! Should be set at 3-1/2 to 4 lbs. of pull, but have NO drag.

12-7   75 meters (plus or minus 5 meters) equals 77 to 87 yards

12-8   James Purdy & Sons

12-9   True

12-10   Change pitch and drop on the stock

12-11   A block of wood, usually walnut to make a gunstock and/or a forearm.

12-12   True! If you fire top barrel first, try firing the bottom barrel first. It worked for me!

12-13   International Skeet targets—higher launch velocity

12-14   98% or better

12-15   False. It reduces "perceived recoil" but no actual rearward movement of the shotgun. The Laws of Physics state it is impossible.

12-16   They were 2-1/2 inches in diameter, smooth and colorless. Later replaced with blue or amber glass.

12-17   True! The International Skeet shooter must also be in a low gun position.

12-18   Wobble trap. It is not sanctioned by ATA, but it is a fun game to shoot.

12-19   Semi-automatics

12-20   Joseph Manton and James Purdy

Questions group 13

13-1   What is the pre-set trajectory of the targets, 10 feet in front of the American Trap house?

13-2   Name three common types of shotgun wooden stock grips.

13-3   **T or F** Swing through, pull away and sustained lead are all three trap shooting approved methods.

13-4   What are the only two ways a shotgun can be carried safely?

13-5   What is the largest size shot you can use in American Trap competitions?

13-6   **T or F** A shooter may repeat any portion of a regularly advertised trap shooting program.

13-7   **T or F** The gauge of the shot shell is printed on every box and every shell.

13-8   A round of trap doubles is how many birds?

13-9   What type of shotgun should not be fired until it has been inspected and approved by a qualified gunsmith?

13-10   _____ _____ is the machining process of reaming or boring, making a larger inside diameter bore in the shotgun barrel.

13-11   **T or F** A shooter should practice in the same shoes or boots that they plan on wearing in a competition.

13-12   Name two popular types of barrel construction for double shotguns.

13-13   Should the beads on the trap barrel's rib be "stacked" in a figure 8, or "side-by-side" for proper alignment?

13-14   **T or F** In a one-day exhibition, Capt. Adam H. Bogardus broke 5,681 glass balls straight, and Annie Oakley broke 4,722 out of 5,000 glass balls.

13-15   Which body part, the feet or your upper body, do you adjust (move) to determine a natural point of aim?

13-16   Which shotgun manufacturer designs his rib with three centered channel grooves, with raised, matted surfaces on the sides?

13-17   What four measurements of the stock are determined by the Try-Gun?

13-18   **T or F** There is no difference on trigger guard tangs between a straight hand or pistol grip stock.

13-19   Where is the finest English walnut for gun stocks grown in the United States?

13-20   Name the two most popular grips (stocks) on a double-trigger side-by-side shotgun.

Answers group 13

13-1   Between 8 and 10 feet high, recommended height is 9 to 9-1/2 feet

13-2   Straight hand grip, "English", semi-pistol or half-pistol grip aka "Prince of Wales" grip, and full pistol grip. There are others, but these are the most popular ones.

13-3   False. They are recognized as sporting clay shooting methods.

13-4   Unloaded in a gun case or open and visibly empty.

13-5   7-1/2 shot

13-6   False. A shooter can ONLY shoot once in an event.

13-7   True! Always check you have the correct ammunition for your gun before firing that first shot.

13-8   50 Birds, 25 Pairs

13-9   A Damascus barrel shotgun

13-10   Back boring

13-11   True! Different shoes or boots could change your sight picture that you had in practice.

13-12   Chopper Lump and Monobloc (Italian term)

13-13   Yes! "Stacked" like a figure eight (8)

13-14   True! Just a fun question about two great early trapshooters

13-15   Your feet. They position your shotgun where you want to aim it.

13-16   SKB, a nice feature

13-17   Cast, drop, pitch and length of pull

13-18   False. Different stocks, different trigger guard tangs

13-19   Northern California, and English walnut is becoming scarce!

13-20   Straight hand stock and "Prince of Wales" stock.

Questions ⬤ group 14

14-1 **T or F** Plastic wads have helped to reduce recoil over the cardboard wad and paper shell.

14-2 What year did the U. S Government outlaw lead shot for waterfowl hunting because of the damage to the ecosphere?

14-3 _____ is a series of holes drilled, laser cut or spark-eroded at angles and shapes near the end of the barrel.

14-4 What controls the shot strings' spread as it leaves the muzzle?

14-5 In handicap trap there shall be not more than ____ yards difference between adjacent shooters in the squad, and no more than a total difference of _____ yards in a squad.

14-6 **T or F** The Olympic Trap clay target is the same diameter as the American Trap target.

14-7 The comment "____ ____" are birds that you broke (hit); "____ ____" are birds you did not break (misses).

14-8 Will a back-bored 12-gauge barrel increase velocity?

14-9 **T or F** As the shot size is increased, the deformity that will occur as it passes through the constriction of the choke will increase.

14-10 Who are considered the "best gun" manufacturers in Germany today?

14-11 What is the approximate time for a trap machine to re-cock its throwing arm?

14-12 How many traps and posts are used in International, Bunker and Olympic Trap?

14-13 What is a "cheek weld?"

14-14 What is a good way to allow you to absorb recoil without losing your balance?

14-15 What is the line called that one follows in space for a clay target?

14-16 **T or F** When shooting International Skeet, you will be required to hold a low gun.

14-17 What is the other common name for an auto-loader?

14-18 Name the three general types of chokes.

14-19 What is a firearm (shotgun) manufactured prior to 1899, by Federal definition, called?

14-20 Shotgun workmanship is described by what two terms?

Answers group 14

14-1 True! Reduced powder load and the sealing off of the bore.

14-2 1992

14-3 Barrel porting

14-4 The choke controls the shot spread

14-5 Two and three

14-6 False. Olympic Trap is 110mm vs. 108mm for American Trap.

14-7 Dead Bird; Lost Bird

14-8 Yes, up to a .740 diameter because you changed the volume of the bore

14-9 True

14-10 Krieghoff and Merkel

14-11 1.8 seconds

14-12 15 traps; three per the five posts

14-13 A "mark" on your cheek from proper gun mounting, same exact place every time.

14-14 A good comfortable stance (foot position), gun point position and proper gun fit

14-15 Trajectory

14-16 True

14-17 Semi-automatic

14-18 Fixed chokes, adjustable chokes and interchangeable chokes

14-19 An antique

14-20 "Fit & Finish"

Questions group 15

15-1   What are the three parts of a plastic wad?

15-2   What is known as a "swarm of bees?"

15-3   The shot charge for Olympic Trap is restricted to what weight limits?

15-4   What range in lengthening, forcing cones, is the most effective from ballistic research?

15-5   **T or F** Porting has virtually no real effect upon the velocity of shot as it leaves the muzzle.

15-6   **T or F** Gratuities are not permitted in skeet competitions.

15-7   What occurs when a shooter is right-handed with left eye dominance or vice versa?

15-8   What year did the American Amateur Trapshooting Association (AATA) disband and start the Amateur Trapshooting Association (ATA)?

15-9   **T or F** White Flyer manufactures two different standard (108m) targets for Eastern and Central U.S. vs. Western states.

15-10 If a trapshooter on post 3 lifts his head "off the stock" on a straightaway target, where will he miss the target?

15-11 Do American Trap and International Skeet shooters usually use the same type and style of shooting vests?

15-12 What style of case do most imported shotgun shell manufacturers use?

15-13 What is the "bore" on a shotgun?

15-14 **T or F** As a general rule for standard chokes, the total range will be between .000 and .045 thousands of an inch under bore diameter.

15-15 What are the terms for the top and bottom edge of a butt plate or recoil pad?

15-16 What was the name of the "charter" when the term "proof" was introduced concerning gun barrel proofing?

15-17 **T or F** In wobble trap, the shooter is allowed two shots at each target?.

15-18 What is a shell bag used for?

15-19 A shotgun's "_____" is determined by the physical dimensions of the butt stock relative to the shooter's physique?

15-20 In International competitions of Olympic Trap, how many targets are shot at by men and women?

Answers group 15

15-1   Powder wad, the cushion and the shotcup

15-2   Your shot string

15-3   24 grams (approximately a 7/8 oz. load)

15-4   1.5 to 1.75 inches

15-5   True. Remember, porting (holes) are near the end of the barrel.

15-6   True, and should not be allowed by the rule book in American Trap or any clay target competitions.

15-7   Cross-eye dominance…shooting problems

15-8   The American Trapshooting Association in 1919, and the Amateur Trapshooting Association (ATA) in 1923. John Phillips Sousa, First President

15-9   True. Good argument about hardness, altitudes and the effects of humidity (see Question 10-20)

15-10   High

15-11   No! Skeet shooters use a slick surface extending down the total vest on the gun mounting side.

15-12   Reifenhauser, a plastic tube

15-13   The inside of the barrel. Normally the dimensions are called by its gauge 12, 16, 20, 28 and 410

15-14   True

15-15   Top edge, heel; bottom edge, toe

15-16   Royal Charter of the London Company of Gunmakers (1637)

15-17   True. The oscillating trap throws some challenging shots.

15-18   To hold spent shells for reloading or just to help keep the field clean. Pick-up after yourself!

15-19   "Fit"

15-20   125 for men; 75 for women

Questions group 16

16-1   What are the three basic types of shotguns used today in the United States?

16-2   **T or F** At first, live birds were shot when released from under "top hats" by pulling the hats off with a string.

16-3   A shooting position in trap is called a _____; in skeet it is called a _____.

16-4   Once the pellets escape the gases and plastic wad, what factor influences the shot charge?

16-5   **T or F** A good shooter will locate the clay target before he moves his gun.

16-6   What is the functional decoration that is cut into the grip and fore-end of your shotgun?

16-7   How big is the shooting square in skeet at each station?

16-8   What makes the loud sound of "BANG!" when a shot is fired?

16-9   What type of shotgun is commonly recommended for beginning youth trap shooters?

16-10   What is the protective plate called that is attached to the butt of the stock?

16-11   Chokes should be cleaned every time the gun is used to eliminate what two problem elements?

16-12   **T or F** Trap layouts, located on country club golf course grounds were popular in the early 1900s.

16-13   What three chokes usually come with a new shotgun (at a minimum)?

16-14   What is the most popular choke combination in Olympic Trap?

16-15   What is the portion of the gun called with all the working parts: the action, trigger, magazine, chamber portion of the barrel?

16-16   What three elements does trapshooting great Kay Ohye say determines consistency in trapshooting?

16-17   Describe the shotgun shooting game of "popinjay?"

16-18   Who was the first shooter in history to win the Grand American Roundhouse?

16-19   Name at least three (or more) international shotgun shell manufacturers.

16-20   What is the major reason to change chokes?

Answers group 16

16-1 Semi-automatic, pump and hinged (usually double barrels), over and under (O/U), or side-by-side

16-2 True. These live bird shooters where known as the "High Hats Club."

16-3 (Trap) post; (skeet) station

16-4 Air resistance (drag) that now influences the pellets.

16-5 True! Good shooting starts with the eyes.

16-6 Checking, usually a pointed pyramid pattern.

16-7 Three foot square. Skeet shooters do move around in the square to set for their shots.

16-8 It is NOT the exploding powder; it is the sound of the shot stream breaking the speed of sound barrier (approximately 768 mph) as it leaves the muzzle of the shotgun.

16-9 12-gauge, automatic with 7/8 oz. or 1 oz. loads will work just fine. 20 gauge is OK in some cases, but it will kick harder and the young shooter might not like the recoil. Try both if you have the chance.

16-10 Butt plate

16-11 Powder residue and plastic fouling build-up

16-12 True! Actually very popular and this was before gated golf course housing communities.

16-13 Full (F), improved cylinder (IC) and modified (M)…and sometimes a skeet (SKT)

16-14 1st barrel (usually lower one) improved modified; 2nd barrel (top) full choke

16-15 The breech

16-16 Shooting style, execution and concentration

16-17 "Popinjay" is a descendant to the pigeon shooting which was a descendant to "clay bird" trapshooting. Popinjay, a live bird tied to the top of a pole with a length of string.

16-18 Kay Ohye, roundhouse is winning them all: Singles, Doubles, Handicap, High Overall and High All Around. WOW!

16-19 ATK/Estate, Fiocchi, Kent/Gamebore, Maxam/RIO and Maxam/Kemen, and there are others.

16-20 To provide the shooter with the largest diameter effective shot string at the distance you are going to break the clay target.

Questions group 17

17-1 **T or F** Famous gun inventor John Browning worked for and invented guns for Winchester.

17-2 Blue rock or "rock" used to name clay pigeons is actually named after what?

17-3 There are seven steps of operation of a shotgun. What is the first step?

17-4 If you sight down the shotgun barrel like a rifle, you will generally shoot where in regards to the clay target?

17-5 Does a larger, brighter front bead increase targets broken in trap and skeet?

17-6 What three initials are usually engraved on the receiver of a double over and under shotgun?

17-7 Demibloc and Monobloc (Italian terminology) makes one think of what type of shotguns?

17-8 By the U.S. Patent Office, when was the first glass ball trap target and clay target introduced to trapshooters?

17-9 Which clay target sport requires American gun club owners to add more facilities?

17-10 Where do "low gun" trapshooters hold their muzzle point before calling for a bird?

17-11 Which shotguns are totally machined from solid steel billets and carry the slogan "shotguns to last a lifetime?"

17-12 Which shotgun manufacturer offers a "triple trigger" system to help adjust the length of pull?

17-13 **T or F** On a double side-by-side shotgun, the distance (measurement) is from the back trigger for the length of pull.

17-14 **T or F** Proper choke tightening is finger tight first, then moderate pressure with the correct fitting wrench.

17-15 What tool helps to determine where the grain will fall, how the color(s) and the figure aspects will compose on a stock?

17-16 What is the recoil-reducing device that mounts on the muzzle to deflect part of the powder gases called?

17-17 What is the most common type of hand engraving encountered on shotguns?

17-18 **T or F** A trapshooter should mount his shotgun across his body (at 45 degrees) rather than square off the shoulder.

17-19 What is the part of the stock that lies under the barrel(s)?

17-20 What is a "shell" magazine loading port?

Answers group 17

17-1   True

17-2   The European blue rock variety of pigeons—comes from early live bird shooting.

17-3   Firing—pulling (or releasing) the trigger, releases the hammer or striker and strikes the shell primer in the chamber.

17-4   Shoot low!

17-5   NO! A shotgun is POINTED, not aimed. You should not be conscious of a front bead.

17-6   "O" over; "U" under and "S" safety. Think initials: OSU or Ohio State University

17-7   Doubles: over and under (O/U) and side-by-side (S/S)

17-8   Glass ball was March 6, 1876; clay target was June 27, 1882

17-9   Olympic (Bunker or International) Trap fields. It is a growing and popular trap game.

17-10   Back edge of the trap house or even slightly lower; "High hun" is held approximately three to four feet above the trap house.

17-11   Ljutic – American-made shotgun

17-12   Browning

17-13   False. Front trigger for proper measurement.

17-14   Absolutely True!

17-15   A transparent template in the generic shape of the stock.

17-16   Compensator or "muzzle brake."

17-17   Scrolls

17-18   True

17-19   The forearm

17-20   A feature where you load the second shell in a pump or automatic shotgun, located underneath the barrel.

Questions group 18

Provided is a gun's trade name (gun name); answer with the shotgun manufacturer's name.

	Trade Name	Shotgun Manufacturer Name
18-1	687-682	
18-2	A-10 American	
18-3	391 Urika	
18-4	XS Skeet	
18-5	F3 American Trap	
18-6	One Touch	
18-7	585	
18-8	BPS	
18-9	90T	
18-10	TM9	
18-11	Model 5	
18-12	K20	
18-13	SuperSport	
18-14	S81	
18-15	Citoris Plus	
18-16	DB81	
18-17	85TTR	
18-18	M2	
18-19	1100	
18-20	Max Performance	

Answers group 18

Shotgun manufacturers

18-1   Beretta

18-2   Connecticut Shotgun

18-3   Beretta

18-4   Browning

18-5   Blaser

18-6   Ljutic

18-7   S K B

18-8   Browning

18-9   Remington

18-10   Perazzi

18-11   Browning

18-12   Krieghoff International

18-13   Benelli

18-14   Silver Seitz

18-15   Browning

18-16   Perazzi (Dan Bonillas model)

18-17   S K B

18-18   Benelli

18-19   Remington

18-20   Kolar

Questions group 19

19-1   How wide is a full choke pattern for a 12-gauge trap shotgun at the normal breaking point of 32 yards?

19-2   What happened in skeet shooting in 1926?

19-3   What was the name of the trophy that DuPont Powder awarded to trapshooters shooting 100 in a row with DuPont Powder?

19-4   What is a barrel guard?

19-5   Name the two shotgun manufacturers that are considered the leaders in International Trap and Skeet competitions today.

19-6   Are there any options for release triggers on over and under (O/U) shotguns?

19-7   **T or F** Ported barrels are allowed in International Skeet competitions.

19-8   Which type of lead? You start with the barrel behind the target, you overtake the target and then fire as you swing through, and get a bit ahead of it.

19-9   What is measured by the number of perfectly spherical balls of lead, each exactly fitting the interior diameter of the barrel, required to make up 16 lbs. in weight?

19-10 **T or F** Bismuth and lead shot can both use the same chokes.

19-11 What are two advantages of a parallel comb that has a neutral cast at the heel?

19-12 What are striker holes?

19-13 When moving from post five to one, which way should the shooter rotate to start moving?

19-14 **T or F** Lead shot is heavier and softer than steel shot.

19-15 _____ is the person who places the clay pigeons on a trap; _____ is the person who releases the clay target from the trap.

19-16 On side-by-side double shotguns with double triggers, which trigger fires which barrel?

19-17 Which post is considered the toughest in trapshooting for right-handed shooters?

19-18 **T or F** A skeet choke (.004 to .005) is designed to place an entire 12-gauge shot charge in a 30" circle at 25 yards.

19-19 What was the "Peoria Blackbird?"

19-20 What shot size is recommended on domed clay birds at 25 yards and beyond?

Answers group 19

19-1   26-plus inches wide

19-2   The sport was named in a contest won by Gertrude Hurlbutt. *Skjuta* (the word "shoot" in Scandinavian) evolved into *skeet.*

19-3   The Du Pont 1915-16 Long Run Trophy—very popular at the time!

19-4   A leather wrap (guard) to protect your hand from "hot barrels"; usually used with side-by-side double shotguns

19-5   Krieghoff International and Perazzi…but others are applying pressure and can quickly change the marketplace

19-6   Yes! You can have release-pull, pull-release and release-release.

19-7   False. NO ported barrels at all.

19-8   Swing-through lead

19-9   Bore size

19-10   True

19-11   Alignment of the shooter's eye to sighting plane does not change, and the recoil of the shotgun does not direct the stock up into the shooter's cheek.

19-12   Holes in the action face where the striker, aka firing pin(s), emerges to detonate the shot shell.

19-13   Rotate, turning to your right to keep muzzle from ever pointing toward other squad members

19-14   True. It also dents easier and has many other characteristics affecting your shot string and pattern.

19-15   Trap boy; puller—can be one and the same

19-16   Front trigger - right barrel; rear trigger - left barrel

19-17   Post #5, the wide left-to-right clay target bird

19-18   True! A very effective choke pattern for skeet.

19-19   The first composition target invented in 1884 by Fred Kimble

19-20   #7-1/2 shot, #8s just lose some of their killing power at 25-plus yards

Questions group 20

20-1 What famous shotgun was nicknamed the "Humpback?"

20-2 What is the force that moves the shotgun backwards into your shoulder when fired?

20-3 **T or F** "Shooting around the clock" is an old, informal term to describe trapshooting posts.

20-4 What two gunsmiths created the boxlock action for Westley-Richards in 1875?

20-5 During World War II, which sport trap or skeet was used to teach airplane gunners the principle of leading a target?

20-6 What is a single projectile shot from a shotgun called?

20-7 What is the difference between "sustained" lead and "maintained" lead?

20-8 What target release system is used in Olympic Trap?

20-9 Name the five basic actions that are available for shotguns.

20-10 An International Skeet shooter with an average of 95% or greater would be in what class?

20-11 What is the distance called from the center line of the stock to the offset, to one side or the other?

20-12 **T or F** Normally, pattern testing for cylinder and skeet chokes in all gauges and all chokes for the .410 bore would occur at 25 yards.

20-13 Does the shot shell speed affect the lead on the target?

20-14 What term do shooters in the United Kingdom and Europe use for shotgun shells?

20-15 What is the minimum legal limit in the United States for a shotgun barrel length?

20-16 What is the largest type of shotgun and what was it used for?

20-17 **T or F** The smaller the number for pellet size and gauge/bore diameter, the larger the size.

20-18 How much does the porting of shotgun barrels increase the decibels of the shot blast?

20-19 What famous shooting instructor developed the Move, Mount and Shoot technique?

20-20 Rate the difficulty from easiest (1) to hardest (7): American Trap, American Skeet, Sporting Clays, Olympic Skeet, FITASC, Olympic Trap and 5-Stand.

Answers group 20

20-1   Browning Automatic 5, (Auto-5; A-5)

20-2   Recoil

20-3   False. It is an old skeet shooting term

20-4   Anson and Deeley. Still a design feature today in several shotguns.

20-5   Skeet

20-6   Slug

20-7   Same meaning—sustained is an American term; maintained is a British term.

20-8   Phono-pull release system to ensure equitable target distribution.

20-9   Break action, pumps, autoloaders (semi-automatics), lever-action and bolt action.

20-10   Master Class (AA)

20-11   Cast

20-12   True

20-13   Yes! With fast shells you will miss in front. With slow shells you will miss behind. Find the shell that works best for you by trying several manufacturers' shot sizes and loads.

20-14   Cartridges

20-15   18″ (457mm) minimum

20-16   "Punt gun" – commercial hunting

20-17   True. Just the opposite of what one would think.

20-18   8db, which is significant!

20-19   Robert Churchill of Great Britain

20-20   Skeet, American Trap, 5-Stand, Olympic Skeet, Sporting Clays, Olympic Trap and FITASC. Now let's start to argue! *(This is the author's opinion.)*

Questions group 21

21-1 What was the first successful and very popular repeating "pump" shotgun?

21-2 Why has the over/under (O/U) shotgun evolved as the gun of choice for most clay target shooters?

21-3 What U.S. President manufactured shot at one time?

21-4 List the gauge diameter in inches of the following; 12-gauge, 20-, 28- and 410.

21-5 What year was the 100th Grand American held at the Vandalia, Ohio home grounds of the ATA?

21-6 Who are the "Big Three" in British shotgun manufacturing?

21-7 What famous actor set two world records in skeet shooting and became a national champion?

21-8 How far in yardage are skeet targets set to fly?

21-9 **T or F** If you want tighter patterns, leave your shells on the dash of your vehicle to sit in the sun to warm-up before shooting.

21-10 Can you measure the choke of a shotgun with a dime?

21-11 Name four types of walnut wood used for shotgun gunstocks.

21-12 **T or F** The ATA regulates the shot shell by velocity instead of by the dram.

21-13 Which type of shotgun normally has a higher stock to raise a shooter's eye to rib level for good visibility?

21-14 At what yardage does #9 shot start to run out of "killing power?"

21-15 If you stop the swing or movement of your shotgun, where will you miss the shot?

21-16 Drop is measured at both _____ and _____ for proper gun fit.

21-17 What is the one thing you look for in the 30" circle when pattern testing?

21-18 What load does ISSF mandate for International Trap?

21-19 **T or F** Shot patterns are normally expressed as a percentage (such as 50%–70%) of all the pellets contained in a shell that strike inside of a circle 30" in diameter at 40 yards.

21-20 What type of rifling is used in the manufacture of shotgun barrels?

Answers group **21**

21-1   Winchester 1887, Model 12 is the most popular

21-2   Weight, less recoil/kick and keeps moving easily once you start it to swing

21-3   Thomas Jefferson, 1774, at the Natural Bridge in the Shenandoah Valley in Virginia

21-4   12-gauge (.729 in.), 20-gauge (.615 in.), 28-gauge (.550 in.) and 410-gauge (.410 in)

21-5   1999

21-6   Boss & Co., Holland & Holland and James Purdy & Sons

21-7   Robert Stack, in movies from 1939–2002, was Eliot Ness in *The Untouchables* and hosted *Unsolved Mysteries* on TV, and various other shows.

21-8   60 yards +/- 2 yards

21-9   True. An old trapshooters secret, but not in the best interest of good sportsmanship!

21-10   No! But old timers will tell you yes! Best way is with dial calipers.

21-11   Black walnut (or American walnut), English walnut, Bastogne walnut and Carlo black walnut

21-12   True – 1290 fps, 12-gauge, 1-1/8 oz., #7-1/2 shot maximum

21-13   Trap shotgun – Monte Carlo stock is a favorite design feature

21-14   At about 25 yards, not a good trap load at all; in American Skeet it is the standard load

21-15   Behind the bird!

21-16   Comb and heel

21-17   Even distribution over the 30" circle. You do not want "holes" which the bird could fly through.

21-18   7/8 oz. (24 gram)

21-19   True

21-20   Shotgun barrels are smooth bore guns, no rifling except some exceptions for shotguns used in hunting with slugs.

Questions group 22

22-1   In what year was the first International Clay Pigeon Tournament contested?

22-2   When a shotgun shooter states his gun is in the "on" position, what is he referring to?

22-3   How many contestants competed in the first Grand American Handicap trap shoot?

22-4   What make and gauge shotgun did "Little Sure Shot" Annie Oakley use in her exhibition shooting?

22-5   What year was the National Skeet Shooting Association (NSSA) formed?

22-6   **T or F** The length of pull is the same for a single trigger double as it is for a two trigger double.

22-7   What is the shooter on post #1 called when a new squad is preparing to shoot a round of trap?

22-8   Which is an easier target for a right hand shooter? Left to right or right to left.

22-9   Why do outstanding shooters in skeet (and sporting clays) round off the top portion of their recoil pad?

22-10   **T or F** A shot gunner properly "squeezes" off a shot from an adjusted trigger.

22-11   Who is the only man to ever win two Grand American Handicaps with live birds?

22-12   **T or F** In Olympic Trap, the shotgun must be unloaded and open during the walk from post #5 back to post #1.

22-13   Which gunsmith patented the first automatic hammerless shotgun?

22-14   **T or F** Like in ball sports, the focus of attention is the ball, never the equipment with which it is to be struck. Shotgun shooting uses this same principle.

22-15   What is an extractor?

22-16   What is "spot shooting?"

22-17   Name the three internal designs of chokes.

22-18   If you raise your head (your eye, the rear sight) as little as 1/8", how far do you change your aim point?

22-19   **T or F** One of the best ways to counter cross wind shooting in trap is to shoot quickly.

22-20   What two leads are involved in a trap shot?

Answers group 22

22-1   May 26–31, 1884 in Chicago under Ligowsky Rules

22-2   The Safety is "ON" which prevents the shotgun (all guns) from firing.

22-3   74. Today, over 5,000 compete for 12 days in August every year.

22-4   Parker, G-grade, 16-gauge

22-5   1946, right after WWII, as a lot of ex-military had trained in skeet during the war.

22-6   False – slight difference, one reason people don't like two triggers

22-7   Squad leader. He shoots first at all five posts.

22-8   Right to left, as you swing your shotgun into your body

22-9   To help in a smoother gun mount without catching one's shooting vest. Some also cover the recoil pad in black vinyl electrical tape to make it more slippery.

22-10 False. A shotgunner "slaps" the trigger firing a shot.

22-11 Thomas Marshall, 1897 and 1899, Trapshooting Hall of Fame member

22-12 True! A very good safety rule and a rules violation in Olympic Trap if shotgun is loaded.

22-13 Daniel Myron LeFever in 1883

22-14 True. Eyes focused on the clay target, never on the shotgun.

22-15 A device that withdraws the fired shotgun shell from the chamber.

22-16 "Spot shooting" is when you think the bird will fly into an area of your shot string.

22-17 Conical parallel, straight conical and wad retarding

22-18 Seven inches at 40 yards, WOW!

22-19 True! If you wait, your point of aim will move outside a 30″ ring with even 10 mph winds.

22-20 Vertical and horizontal leads

Questions group 23

Provided is a gun's trade name (gun name); answer with the shotgun manufacturer's name.

	Trade Name	Shotgun Manufacturer Name
23-1	K-80	
23-2	DT10	
23-3	IMPACT	
23-4	BT-99	
23-5	FB	
23-6	SX3	
23-7	Empire II	
23-8	101	
23-9	MX-8, MX-15	
23-10	Model 21	
23-11	Cynergy	
23-12	686 Silver Pigeon	
23-13	870	
23-14	Superposed	
23-15	RBL Sporting Edition	
23-16	85TSS	
23-17	A400 Xplor	
23-18	D.T.S.	
23-19	Model 12	
23-20	Citori XT	

Answers group 23

Shotgun manufacturers

23-1   Krieghoff International

23-2   Beretta "Detachable Trigger"

23-3   Caesar Guerini

23-4   Browning

23-5   Blaser

23-6   Winchester – automatic – 12 shots in 1.442 seconds

23-7   Charles Daly

23-8   Winchester

23-9   Perazzi

23-10   Winchester (originally) now Connecticut Shotgun

23-11   Browning with Reverse Striker Trigger System

23-12   Beretta

23-13   Remington

23-14   Browning

23-15   Connecticut Shotgun

23-16   S K B

23-17   Beretta

23-18   Caeser Guerini "Dynamic Tuning System"

23-19   Winchester

23-20   Browning

Questions group 24

24-1   On which type of shotgun is the fore-end connected to the beech-bolt by rods called "action bars?"

24-2   Who was the first shooter to have a .9900 singles average?

24-3   Who has the responsibility to check the scores after each round of 25, the squad leader or the individual shooter?

24-4   What yardage in handicap trap is considered "back-yardage?"

24-5   In handicap trapshooting, from 18 through 20 yards is called what position?

24-6   **T or F** Ported barrels are permitted in Olympic Trap.

24-7   At what height do the clay targets come out of the high and low houses in skeet?

24-8   A "Slide Action" shotgun is better known as a _____ shotgun.

24-9   If the safety mechanism shows "red," is the safety on or off?

24-10 Name the following shotgun shooting organizations: ATA, NSSA, NRA and NSSF.

24-11 In skeet, when shooting singles, the bird comes from which house first?

24-12 **T or F** In Olympic Trap, each shooter gets two lefts, two rights and one straightaway, and no randomized target angles from each post.

24-13 In skeet, how far apart is each station with #8 centered between the high and low houses?

24-14 _____ is any trap shooter who has not reached his or her 18th birthday.

24-15 Who were Thompson-Oberfell?

24-16 **T or F** The radius of a pistol grip and the length of pull (trigger) determines the positioning of the shooter's hand affecting both control and comfort.

24-17 What is billed as the "World's Largest Shooting Event?"

24-18 **T or F** A good walnut stock that has been air-dried for two years will probably not crack on you.

24-19 _____ is the term used for the operating mechanism of a shotgun.

24-20 Describe a "Drilling" shotgun.

Answers group 24

24-1   Pump shotguns

24-2   A.J. Stauber from Los Angeles, California, 1927 with an average of .9905

24-3   The individual shooter must check his scores!

24-4   24 to 27 yards

24-5   Low yardage

24-6   False

24-7   High House – 10 feet; Low House – 3-1/2 feet

24-8   Pump action shotgun

24-9   "OFF," it is ready to fire!

24-10   ATA Amateur Trapshooting Association of America, NSSA National Skeet Shooting
        Association, NRA National Rifle Association, NSSF National Shooting Sports
        Foundation

24-11   High House

24-12   True

24-13   26 feet, 8 inches in the semi-circle layout

24-14   Junior

24-15   Patterning Gurus, wrote famous book titled *Mysteries of Shotgun Patterns*

24-16   True

24-17   The Grand American World Trap Shooting Championships, held each August at the
        World Shooting and Recreational Complex in Sparta, Illinois

24-18   True. Time to air-dry a nice piece of wood is critical.

24-19   Action

24-20   A "drilling" has three barrels, two of the same gauge shotgun and the third a rifle
        barrel. A Vierling is a combination of four barrels. Both guns are known as
        "combination guns."

Questions   group 25

25-1   How many traps were used in the original "Glass Ball" trap contests?

25-2   What countries do the following shotguns come from: Purdy & Sons, Beretta, Perazzi, Holland and Holland, Kreighoff International and Boss & Co.?

25-3   A dram equivalent measurement on a shotgun shell is equal to how many ounces of black powder?

25-4   Which target is harder to break, an edge-on target or a target with its belly exposed?

25-5   What four gauges are shot in American Skeet?

25-6   **T or F** Trapshooters may use shells they have reloaded with black powder in competition.

25-7   What year was the first known 100 straight shot in trap with Ligowsky targets?

25-8   What four points of your body does a shotgun touch?

25-9   What is the minimum height and maximum height for Olympic Trap targets as measured 10 meters in front of the bunker?

25-10   **T or F** The depth of a crimp on your shotgun shell can affect the ballistics significantly.

25-11   **T or F** A right-hand shooter with a "blocky" face would probably "cast off" to the right.

25-12   Where is the "tubular magazine" located on a pump shotgun?

25-13   Who manufactures the shotgun nicknamed "The Nostalgia Gun?"

25-14   Since most shots in shotgun sports are taken under 40 yards, which choke is considered the best all-around one?

25-15   What function does a wheel thumb perform?

25-16   Name the four parts that make up a box lock action made famous by gunsmiths Anson & Deeley in 1875.

25-17   **T or F** The break action shotgun is the easiest shotgun to maintain and is generally the safest.

25-18   Do all chokes perform the same for all loads made by the same manufacturer?

25-19   What distances do shooters shoot at post #1 and #5, and #2 and #4 when shooting wobble trap?

25-20   When under stress in a competition, what one move can you make to ease the stress and re-establish your shooting style?

Answers group 25

25-1   Three, 1 left, 1 straight and 1 right – shot at 18 yards

25-2   England, Italy, Italy, England, Germany and England

25-3   1/16th on an ounce

25-4   Edge-on

25-5   12-gauge (most popular), 20, 28 and 410

25-6   False. Never!

25-7   1880 by Rolla Heikes, he also won the first Grand American Handicap in 1900

25-8   Your two hands, your cheek and your shoulder pocket

25-9   Minimum 1.5 meters to 3.5 meters maximum

25-10   True – velocity and pressure

25-11   True. A skinny, narrow face would probably "cast on" to the left.

25-12   Underneath the barrel, on which the pump-sliding forearm handle sides working the action

25-13   Ithaca Model 37, 16-gauge

25-14   Modified as its pattern is very effective at 35-40 yards with 45%-55% within a 30" circle at 40 yards.

25-15   To move and/or adjust the adjustable ribs

25-16   Cocking lever, main spring, tumbler and sear

25-17   True

25-18   No! Best to always pattern all loads with all chokes.

25-19   #1 & #5 posts – 18 yards; #2 & #4 posts – 17 yards

25-20   Step back and take a deep breath! Remember "mental interruptions" mean misses.

Questions ◉ group 26

26-1　**T or F** The first ten Grand Americans were shot at live pigeons.

26-2　**T or F** Shooting posts in Olympic Trap are in a straight line.

26-3　Which term is more correct, automatic or autoloader, when you must pull the trigger for each shot?

26-4　**T or F** A screw-in choke tube will pattern differently from one shotgun to another.

26-5　How far apart are the five shooting posts in American Trap?

26-6　**T or F** In American Skeet doubles, if you break both birds with one shot ("Annie Oakley") you have to re-shoot them both.

26-7　Which gauge is the most "nostalgic gauge" in shotguns today?

26-8　What does air drying do for walnut gun stocks and fore-ends?

26-9　What is the typical barrel length for a trap gun and a skeet gun in America today?

26-10　**T or F** In wobble trap, shooters can use skeet positions to shoot the game.

26-11　What is the exit speed of the bird in International Trap?

26-12　**T or F** A "Golden Rule" when you get a broken bird: do not stand with the gun mounted and say "pull" again.

26-13　Name the three methods of operating actions to increase the rate of fire of a shotgun.

26-14　The shotgun nicknamed "The Platonic Ideal" is manufactured by whom?

26-15　Who is the official supplier of trap machines for the ATA in Sparta, Illinois?

26-16　What facility is mandatory to visit for the history of shotguns, documents and artifacts in Birmingham, England?

26-17　What is easier to do, come up on a target or drop down on the target?

26-18　Name the five specifications listed on a typical shot shell box.

26-19　When you pattern your trap shotgun, how many times do you fire at the pattern sheet?

26-20　Which type of double shotgun is favored for upland bird shooting vs. clay targets?

Answers group 26

26-1   True. 1893–1902 shot at Dexter Park, Long Island, New York

26-2   True. Not curved like an American Trap Field, 15 meters (16-1/2 yards)

26-3   Autoloader and automatic is a misnomer, but used interchangeably.

26-4   True! Always pattern your shotgun to get to know where it shoots with particular chokes and loads.

26-5   Posts are three yards apart

26-6   True

26-7   16-gauge and growing in popularity once again!

26-8   Minimizes internal fracturing and enhances the integrity of the wood. 7% moisture content is the goal.

26-9   Trap shotgun 30″/32″, tight choke, full or modified; Skeet shotgun 26″/28″ open skeet choke

26-10   True, but usually done by more experienced shooters.

26-11   International Trap is 62 mph (100 km/h); American Trap is 40 mph (64 km/h)

26-12   False! Always dismount and start your shooting procedure all over again.

26-13   Semi-automatics use inertia, gas or recoil to increase the rate of fire.

26-14   James Purdy & Sons

26-15   Pat-traps

26-16   The Birmingham Gun Barrel Proof House, Banbury Street, Birmingham, England

26-17   Coming up! Your barrel won't block your vision of the target if you are below the flight line.

26-18   Gauge, length of the shell, shot size, weight in ounces of shot, dram equivalent and quantity (25).

26-19   One time ONLY. Each time you shoot a pattern, but shoot a minimum of five pattern target sheets.

26-20   Side-by-side because it is a lighter and smaller shotgun.

Questions ![clay target icon] group 27

27-1 State the approximate number of #8 and #7-1/2 shot in the following loads: 7/8 oz., 1 oz. and 1-1/8 oz.

27-2 What is the firearms industry's most trusted reference book with over 1.3 million copies in print?

27-3 **T or F** Porting increases the amount of noise heard by the shooter and others nearby.

27-4 What shot size range is allowed in American Skeet?

27-5 _____ is the percentage of targets the shooter in American Trap has hit out of the total shot at. Used for handicapping and classifying purposes.

27-6 Which clay target standard is used in Olympic Trap and Olympic Skeet competitions?

27-7 What trophy is awarded for the most gold medals in the World Shooting Championships?

27-8 Where are the U.S. Olympic Trap and Olympic Skeet teams located for training?

27-9 **T or F** Modern over/under (O/U) shotguns may be vented top and bottom (between barrels) as a design feature.

27-10 If you start to re-check your lead to be certain of it, what happens?

27-11 **T or F** When a shooter changes any one component—shells, hard for soft shot, short charges, wads, primers or powders—they should pattern their shotgun for sure.

27-12 **T or F** A shooter can affect the shape of a shot string (and pattern) with a very quick swing.

27-13 What was the first successful semi-automatic shotgun and who designed it?

27-14 The shotgun nicknamed "The Desert Island Gun" is manufactured by whom?

27-15 Without question, the eyes are the most important factor in breaking targets; what is the major factor that causes many misses?

27-16 **T or F** In skeet, under no circumstances shall the result of firing upon a broken target be scored.

27-17 Name the two types of mechanisms side-by-side shotguns are designed and built around.

27-18 A semi-automatic is more difficult to maintain than a break-action shotgun like an over/under (O/U), but it is known for what shooting feature?

27-19 "Trap etiquette" is very important to trap shooters, name a few examples!

27-20 What does SCTP stand for?

Answers group 27

27-1   #8: 7/8 oz. (359), 1oz. (410) and 1-1/8 (462)
       #7-1/2: 7/8 oz. (306), 1 oz. (350) and 1-1/8 (393)

27-2   *Blue Book of Gun Values,* 30th edition in print 2010. A great price guide book!

27-3   True. One of the big cons against ported barrels.

27-4   No shot smaller than #9 or larger than #7-1/2 in any load.

27-5   Average

27-6   International targets (110mm, weight 105 grams +/- tolerances)

27-7   Nasser Trophy (1st awarded by President Gamal Nasser of Egypt, 1962)

27-8   Olympic Training Center (OTC) in Colorado Springs, Colorado

27-9   True

27-10 Your swing slows down or even stops and you will miss the bird.

27-11 True. Results can be very extreme and very surprising

27-12 False. Shot string moving too fast, i.e. at 1250 fps the shot string at the muzzle leaves at 1/15,000 of a second.

27-13   Browning A-5, designed by John Browning

27-14 Remington 870 - best selling shotgun of all time

27-15 Gun fit. Get it right and there will be immediate improvement in your scores, and remember to never stop swinging (moving) your shotgun.

27-16 True. Also true in American Trap and sporting clays.

27-17 Box-lock and side-lock

27-18 Lower recoil

27-19 Shell catchers on automatics, no chatting, no yelling, no picking-up dropped shells until you move to next post, no blowing smoke out of the barrel(s)—nothing that will disturb a squad's rhythm

27-20 Scholastic Clay Target Program: A great program to help young trapshooters

Questions   group 28

28-1   Which type of shotgun is the best-selling double-barreled shotgun in the world today?

28-2   Which powder produces greater power, old black powders or modern smokeless powders?

28-3   Which type of shot, lead or steel, has a longer shot string?

28-4   When (in what year) was the first time a trap shooter reached the 27-yard line in handicap?

28-5   **T or F** If the length of pull is too short, making it hard to apply proper trigger pressure, it may also cause flinching.

28-6   **T or F** A trap or skeet squad with a "shooting rhythm" is preferred vs. one with a lot of motion, noise and interruptions.

28-7   Which shotgun manufacturer makes a shotgun with adjustable point of impact from 50/50 to 90/10 by turning a wheel located in the muzzle support?

28-8   What does a chronograph perform?

28-9   **T or F** Sounds above 90 decibels can permanently damage your auditory nerves.

28-10   What is the suggested number of times you test pattern for every choke and/or shot shell you shoot with?

28-11   Name the two gauges (bores in U.K.) of the following dimensions: (0.614 in, 15.6mm) and (0.729 in, 18.5mm).

28-12   What is a "void" in a pattern sheet?

28-13   The shotgun nicknamed "The Aristocrat" is manufactured by whom?

28-14   What do baseball, tennis, shotgun shooting, football, basketball and lacrosse all have in common?

28-15   **T or F** In skeet, you should start to move your gun upon your call of "pull" to get ahead of the target.

28-16   A matching single barrel and a double barrel set of over/under (O/U) barrels are called what?

28-17   What are the standard dimensions of the standard clay (bird) target used for American Trap and American Skeet?

28-18   Which clay target shooting sport has a "Target Crossing Point?"

28-19   Why do trapshooters wear "blinders?"

28-20   Who is the largest manufacturer of screw-in chokes in the United States?

Answers group 28

28-1 Over and under (O/U)

28-2 Modern day smokeless powders

28-3 Lead: The steel shot string might be 1/2 the length and 60% narrower diameter

28-4 February 12, 1955; two shooters - Stockdale and Rieggor at Las Vegas Gun Club

28-5 True

28-6 True. Absolutely, or your scores may go down! It's all about etiquette.

28-7 S K B

28-8 A chronograph is an electronic machine that measures the speed of moving objects through the air...like shot shell pellets.

28-9 True! Ear protection is mandatory whenever shooting shotgun sports.

28-10 Five times minimum for good results, ten times is much better!

28-11 20-gauge; 12-gauge

28-12 A portion of the pattern sheet where a clay target silhouette will fit and not cover three or more holes is a problem.

28-13 Browning – Superposed Model

28-14 They all require hand and eye coordination along with proper training/coaching to hit or catch the desired object.

28-15 False. Do just the opposite, move the gun once you establish the target with your eyes.

28-16 Combo

28-17 1/8″ thick, 4-5/l6″ (108mm) diameter, weight 3.5 ounces (95 grams to 105 grams +/- 5 grams) and 1-1/8″ (1.1″ to 1.3″) height

28-18 Skeet, a point for target flights from both the high and low house to cross.

28-19 To block viewing other shooters movement and also to block the sun.

28-20 Briley Manufacturing

Questions group 29

29-1 Who was the first U.S. President to be an avid shotgunner?

29-2 When was trapshooting first mentioned in a sporting-type magazine?

29-3 What is a snap cap?

29-4 **T or F** There are no major clay shooting events in the U.S. or Europe that include 16-gauge shotguns.

29-5 Which state grows the greatest variety and diversity of walnut used for shotgun gunstocks?

29-6 Which gauge is primarily a skeet gauge and has limited usage?

29-7 **T or F** Your left arm (RH shooters) should form an angle of 45 degrees to the side of the shotgun for maximum ease in vertical and horizontal movement.

29-8 What is the world's most popular clay target game by volume today?

29-9 Which trap posts does the shooter's muzzle set-up either slightly left or right of the trap house centerline?

29-10 What causes more misses than all other reasons combined?

29-11 What is the distance called between the single trigger and the center of the gun butt?

29-12 What two types of shotguns have a "point of convergence" (POC) where both barrels shoot to the same spot?

29-13 What fitting system is used on SKB 85TSS gun stocks?

29-14 What was the first lever action shotgun and who designed it?

29-15 Which shotgun shooting method just doesn't work in American Trap shooting?

29-16 Describe a Monte Carlo gun stock.

29-17 In skeet, the optional shot after running the first 24 shall be taken from which station?

29-18 Which grip design keeps the palms of your hands on the same plane...which helps to keep elbows up and away from your body.

29-19 Name the three types (methods) of barrel joining in side-by-side double shotguns.

29-20 What was the last great John Browning shotgun? It was designed before he died and became the most popular double barrel in the United States.

Answers group 29

29-1 President Theodore Roosevelt. He loved his A.H. Fox shotgun.

29-2 1793, in an English magazine, *Sporting Magazine.* Trap is our oldest shot gunning sport.

29-3 A device that appears to be a standard shotgun shell with no primer or projectile, but is used to dry-fire one's shotgun.

29-4 True! At one time it was the second most popular gauge, today it is a credible gauge and has high profile marketing opportunities.

29-5 California, because nuts were planted and cross-pollinated.

29-6 410-gauge

29-7 True. A greater angle would inhibit vertical movement, while a lesser angle inhibits horizontal movement.

29-8 American Trap, but sporting clays continue to grow in popularity and volume of shooting targets. One should also watch the growth in Olympic (bunker) Traps and ZZ Bird Helice layouts.

29-9 Post #3, to avoid the barrel blocking (not seeing the blur) on a straightaway shot.

29-10 Lifting one's head! A head movement of 1/4″ equates to a missed shot by 9″ at the common 32-yard breaking point in trap.

29-11 Length of pull

29-12 Over and under (O/U) and side-by-side doubles...we hope they shoot the same spot!

29-13 Graco "CTS" System that allows the shooter to adjust the comb for both height and offset (cast)

29-14 Winchester M1887, designed by John Browning

29-15 Maintained lead or sustained lead

29-16 A stock with an elevated comb

29-17 Station #8, shooting the low house only

29-18 English Grip

29-19 Demi-Bloc, Chopper Lump and Monobloc

29-20 Browning Superposed (B-25)

Questions group 30

30-1   What type of shotgun is designed with a high rib to assist shooting a rising target?

30-2   The _____ is the narrow portion of the stock held with the trigger hand.

30-3   Targets thrown at distances and angles which do not meet the specifications in the rulebook are called what?

30-4   For a novice trapshooter, what are some of the more important things an experienced trapshooter can teach?

30-5   What is the most highly-prized and sought after gunstock wood?

30-6   What is the maximum shot size and load for International Skeet?

30-7   **T or F** A shot gunner's hips need to be free to pivot, like a golfer, to help drive the body into a shot.

30-8   What is the biggest problem for new shotgun shooters?

30-9   What does the icon (SAMMI) stand for in the USA?

30-10   The shotgun nicknamed "Soft Shooter" is manufactured by whom?

30-11   **T or F** Inertia trigger systems will function when dry firing is practiced.

30-12   How far are birds thrown in International Skeet?

30-13   What is the difference between a side-lock and a side-plate shotgun?

30-14   Where is the National Trapshooting Hall of Fame and Museum located?

30-15   What is the key number of registered trap targets to have been shot after November 1st each year to not be re-classified at the Grand American or other events if no previous history?

30-16   What does a red flag or an orange traffic cone on top of a trap house mean to all shooters?

30-17   Name three major golf winners who liked to shoot shotguns at clay targets and hunt upland birds?

30-18   What is a good way to describe the right amount of grip pressure?

30-19   Between a #7-1/2 or #8 shot, which one drops less, carries a higher energy factor and its arrival time is faster when measured at 60 yards at 1200 feet per second?

30-20   If you see some rib in between the beads and pointing in an upward direction when looking down your trap barrel, where will you shoot?

Answers group 30

30-1   Trap gun

30-2   Grip

30-3   Illegal targets – shooter is allowed to refuse and call for another target

30-4   Trapshooting etiquette

30-5   English thin-shelled walnut—it is also the most expensive.

30-6   7/8 oz., #7-1/2 shot

30-7   True. Think pivot, but under control.

30-8   Consistent gun mounting and practice, practice, practice...practice and practice some more.

30-9   Sporting Arms and Ammunition Manufacturers Institute

30-10   Remington Model 1100

30-11   False. The system requires recoil of an actual shot to index the second trigger.

30-12   72 meters

30-13   Side-lock: the lock mechanisms are built on separate plates, fixed to the wood, immediately behind the action. Sideplate: a conventional box-lock, all firing mechanisms mounted within the action.

30-14   The new one is located at the World Shooting & Recreational Complex in Sparta, Illinois.

30-15   1,000 registered targets

30-16   Stop shooting, unload shotguns until situation is fixed, or trap house is re-opened for shooting.

30-17   Bobby Jones, Tom Watson and Jack Nicklaus

30-18   Imagine you are holding raw eggs in your hands. Think about relaxing your hands, which will help you move more freely.

30-19   # 7-1/2 shot

30-20   You will shoot over your target and miss!

Questions group 31

31-1   Which type of shotgun uses the energy of the first shot to re-cock the gun for the next shot?

31-2   Which clay target manufacturer makes pink clays to support the fight against breast cancer?

31-3   Name the three types of triggers.

31-4   At what stations do skeet shooters shoot two singles (one low, one high house) and a pair of doubles in a round of 25 birds?

31-5   What common choke restrictions do you see on Olympic Trap shotguns because of 7/8 oz. load limitations?

31-6   **T or F** In all American Trap games, each shooter is allowed only one shot per target.

31-7   What does "shooting range equals 70% pattern density" mean?

31-8   How many degrees, left to right, do the trap machines oscillate in American Trap?

31-9   The shotgun nicknamed "The Machine Age Marvel" is manufactured by whom?

31-10   How high (in feet) are skeet targets at the center stake?

31-11   **T or F** "Fear the angles, but miss the straight-aways." (an old saying)

31-12   To raise the center of impact (of your pattern) does one use more or less drop at the comb?

31-13   When cleaning your shotgun, should you use grease or gun oil?

31-14   **T or F** No right-handed trap shooter can swing as far to the right of center as they can to the left.

31-15   Where is the safety located on a semi-automatic or pump shotgun?

31-16   Name the five stages of the firing sequence of a shot shell.

31-17   Which semi-automatic sends the spent hull downward with a bottom-ejection system?

31-18   Who is the oldest and largest shotgun manufacturer in Turkey?

31-19   What is a "thumbhole?"

31-20   Give an example of cross-eye dominance.

Answers group 31

31-1   Automatic or autoloader

31-2   White Flyer – A great target for fundraising

31-3   Inertia, mechanical and release triggers

31-4   Stations one, two, six and seven

31-5   First barrel (0.64 - 0.72mm) (0.025 -0.030 inches); second barrel (0.80-1.00mm) (0-032 -0.040 inches)

31-6   True, be it singles, doubles or handicap

31-7   The choke you should use to get these results (70%) - Skeet-1 choke for skeet or full choke for trap are good examples of correct shooting range "killing" distance.

31-8   35 degrees (17.5 degrees each way from center)

31-9   Winchester – Model 12

31-10 15 feet above the ground on a level field

31-11 True. Trapshooters miss more straightaway targets then angles, especially on post #3.

31-12 Less drop at the comb

31-13 Both, oil for lubrication, grease for lugs—do not over-apply either one.

31-14 True. Learn to adjust your stance to help your swing to reach 180 degrees

31-15 In the trigger guard

31-16 (1) Firing pin hits primer, (2) primer ignites, (3) powder ignites, (4) burning powder forms gases, (5) expanding hot gases propel wad and shot down the barrel

31-17 Beretta UGB25 Xcel – very user-friendly when on the line

31-18 Huglu

31-19 A hole in the stock. It's about the grip to assist in one's grip. Not a very popular feature.

31-20 A shooter doesn't shoulder his gun under his dominant eye. Example: left eye dominate shooter, shoots from the right shoulder

Questions group 32

32-1 **T or F** A launched broken target that is shot at and hit is scored as a dead bird in trap.

32-2 When a shooter talks about a "Fence Post," what is he referring to?

32-3 What shotgun feature determines which barrel of a double barrel shotgun will fire first?

32-4 What is a "Shell Knocker?"

32-5 Which type of lead? You start ahead of the target to begin with, adjust your lead and fire.

32-6 What does the term "getting a punch" mean?

32-7 **T or F** One should always bring the shotgun up to their face, rather than lowering their face down onto the shotgun comb.

32-8 What is the raised sighting plane affixed to the top of a barrel?

32-9 The shotgun nicknamed "The Unbreakable Gun" is manufactured by whom?

32-10 **T or F** When purchasing a shotgun it is important to be familiar with the gun laws in your state.

32-11 As a trapshooter, how much of your pattern do you want above the bulls-eye?

32-12 Which gauge is becoming popular once again because of its many benefits and features?

32-13 **T of F** In American Skeet, the shooter may pre-mount the shotgun, while in Olympic Skeet one must hold a low gun.

32-14 Which Formula One World Champion racecar driver won the British, Welsh and Scottish Skeet Championships, plus the 'Coupe de Nations' European Championship?

32-15 **T or F** The difference between a good trapshooter and a great one is ultimately decided by the mental game of trapshooting.

32-16 Name the four human factors that affect a shot gunner's ability to shoot.

32-17 On shotguns with adjustable triggers for length of pull from the pistol grip, how much travel is offered for total adjustment?

32-18 What is the subconscious mind resisting when subjecting the body to another recoil blow?

32-19 Why do most movies usually have all the actors using side-by-side shotguns?

32-20 "Rifles are _____; shotguns are _____."

Answers group 32

32-1   False. A shooter must break a whole target to be scored a dead bird.

32-2   Bad/ugly-looking wood on the stock of a shotgun

32-3   "Barrel Selector" or "Selector Systems"

32-4   Usually a solid brass pin about four inches long with a diameter smaller than a 20-gauge. Used to knock stuck wads out of a shotgun barrel.

32-5   Sustained lead or maintained lead

32-6   In American Handicap Trap, when a shooter shoots 96 or higher, or earns yardage in a competition, they get a "punch" and next time they shoot further back from the trap house, up to 27 yards.

32-7   True! Lowering your face causes several shooting problems.

32-8   Rib

32-9   Winchester Model 21

32-10   True. Gun laws vary from one state to another. Get to know your state's requirements.

32-11   60% minimum normally. Remember, you are shooting a rising target

32-12   16-gauge, as it is a great fit between a 12-gauge and a 20-gauge

32-13   True

32-14   Scottish shooter, Jackie Stewart. Visit his facility at the Gleneagles Hotel in Scotland.

32-15   True! Some shooting instructors say it is over 90% of the game.

32-16   Psychology, fitness, vision and nutrition

32-17   3/8"

32-18   Flinching

32-19   I don't know the answer, maybe it is just Hollywood, but this is a question for lots of discussion.

32-20   Rifle: aimed; shotgun: pointed. Know the difference and why!

Questions group 33

33-1 Glass balls that were stuffed with feathers or powder, giving an illusion of a bird being hit when broken, were called what?

33-2 _____ is the signal given by the shooter to release a clay target.

33-3 Which London gun maker introduced a lower-priced box-lock shotgun honoring famous gun maker John Robertson in 2009?

33-4 **T or F** International Skeet targets fly the same distance as American Skeet clay targets.

33-5 What is the most popular length barrel for skeet?

33-6 What is a "flash" target?

33-7 **T or F** If the drop at the comb is too low it will cause the wrong eye to take over (cross-eye dominance).

33-8 **T or F** Auto-loading shotguns are not allowed in Olympic Trap competitions.

33-9 Which American shotgun is considered the "best of all" by gunsmiths and gun writers?

33-10 When and where was the first women's trap club established?

33-11 What are the two "special categories" regarding ATA Youth Shooters?

33-12 What is the "elevator" on a specific type of shotgun?

33-13 What is one of the critical factors that determine if a clay target will break if hit with just a few pellets?

33-14 How are interchangeable chokes secured in the shotgun barrel?

33-15 The shotgun nicknamed "The Birmingham Box" is manufactured by whom?

33-16 What happens when a shooter with a well-rounded face or large cheeks using a high-combed gun and neutral cast, shoots?

33-17 Who developed the box-lock action?

33-18 Which type of shotgun has fewer moving parts, thus less maintenance, a pump or a semi-automatic?

33-19 In doubles trap, the target shall be thrown not less than _____ yards nor more than _____ yards.

33-20 **T or F** 16-gauge is a permitted gauge in American Skeet, but not in Olympic Skeet.

Answers group 33

33-1   "Puff balls"

33-2   "Pull" is the usual signal call, but any sound will suffice.

33-3   Boss & Co.

33-4   False. 70 yards, because of faster target speed.

33-5   28″ long

33-6   A clay target with a pouch of fluorescent-colored powder underneath or on top of the dome. With a "kill," the target provides a puff of colored smoke.

33-7   True! This is why this adjustment is so important in gun fitting.

33-8   True! Over and under (O/U) is the most popular shotgun.

33-9   Winchester Model 21

33-10   July 1913 at The Nemours Gun Club, Wilmington, Delaware by Miss Harriet Hammond. More women may have shot trap than played golf at the time!

33-11   Sub-Junior Class: not yet 15 years old; Junior Class: those who have not turned 18 years old

33-12   Pump shotguns, the lever which pushes the shotgun shell forward into the chamber by the bolt.

33-13   The amount of centrifugal spin rate ("rotation") of the clay bird. The faster they spin, the easier they are to break.

33-14   Screwing the choke into the threaded portion of the barrel. Snug, but not real tight is best.

33-15   Westley Richards & Co.

33-16   His face pushes the stock down and to the right, causing the shotgun to shoot high and to the left.

33-17   Anson & Deeley; William Anson and John Deeley both worked for Westley Richards & Co.

33-18   Pump

33-19   44 yards to 51 yards, a little different from singles

33-20   False. Permitted gauges are 12, 20, 28, 410, but you could shoot your 16-gauge for fun and practice.

Questions   group 34

Name the country where the shotgun was originally manufactured.

	Shotgun Manufacturer	**Country of Manufacture**
34-1	Boss & Co.	
34-2	Browning (USA)	
34-3	Armas Garbi	
34-4	James Purdy & Sons	
34-5	Krieghoff International	
34-6	Remington	
34-7	Perazzi	
34-8	Ithaca	
34-9	F.lli Rizzini	
34-10	Holland & Holland	
34-11	Browning (Europe)	
34-12	Lebeau-Courally	
34-13	Beretta	
34-14	L.C. Smith	
34-15	Parker	
34-16	Winchester	
34-17	Piotti Fratelli	
34-18	Westley Richards	
34-19	A.H. Fox	
34-20	SKB	

Answers group 34

Country of Manufacture

34-1 England

34-2 United States of America

34-3 Spain

34-4 England

34-5 Germany

34-6 United States of America

34-7 Italy

34-8 United States of America

34-9 Italy

34-10 England

34-11 Belgium

34-12 Belgium

34-13 Italy

34-14 United States of America

34-15 United States of America

34-16 United States of America

34-17 Italy

34-18 England

34-19 United States of America

34-20 Japan

Questions 🪙 group 35

35-1   What is the term for the number of targets a shooter loses from a perfect score in trap?

35-2   Who is considered by many experts to be London's greatest gun maker?

35-3   A shotgun barrel (an older one or antique) with fine, wavy lines (which you can see) might be what type of barrel?

35-4   **T or F** Back boring will help reduce the length of a shot string.

35-5   What two historical events introduced shotguns to the general public?

35-6   _____ is the end of the barrel nearest the gun stock.

35-7   When was/is "The Golden Age of Shotgunning?"

35-8   For what type of shotgun were release triggers originally designed?

35-9   What type of shotgun has a stock that has been cut into several pieces and put back together with adjusting screws and gears?

35-10   How does one prevent "fixed guns repaired?"

35-11   In Great Britain, Australia and South America, what form of trap shooting is popular?

35-12   What is one of the best ways to practice your gun mount?

35-13   What type of shotgun is recommended to teach beginning (novice) shooters under supervision?

35-14   How much constriction do "cylinder barrels" have from the shotgun manufacturer?

35-15   **T or F** In English Skeet vs. American Skeet, the shooter shoots a double on station four instead of singles from station eight.

35-16   When and where was the first night trapshooting event in the United States?

35-17   **T or F** The way choke constriction slows the wad usually determines how the shot passes from the muzzle to encompass air resistance.

35-18   What do the following initials stand for: HOA and HAA?

35-19   What common mistake do golfers and shotgun shooters both make?

35-20   In American Handicap Trap, should the shooter hold his normal position or one that is higher or lower?

Answers group 35

35-1   Down, i.e. 72 out of a 75 (Down 3 going into last round of 25)

35-2   James Purdy & Sons – but this is open to argument

35-3   Damascus – never shoot it until it is inspected and approved by a qualified gunsmith

35-4   True, because you will have a large center mass in the shot string.

35-5   World War I and World War II, automatic and pump shotguns became very popular.

35-6   The breech

35-7   Today! The present times offer a great selection of shotguns, equipment and accessories, and shotgun shooting sports are expanding with new gun clubs and facilities. Enjoy!

35-8   Single-shot trap shotguns

35-9   Try-Gun, to help determine proper gun fit

35-10   Clean and lubricate your shotgun properly after every use.

35-11   Down-the Line (DTL): Two shots allowed, three points for first-barrel hit, and two points for second-barrel hit

35-12   In a mirror, check out your head and eyes along with your arm positions

35-13   Pump, so student can keep a grip on the shotgun and concentrate on proper gun handling and preparing for the next shot

35-14   NO constriction at all!

35-15   True

35-16   June 10, 1880 at the Orion Gun Club, Philadelphia, Pennsylvania

35-17   True!

35-18   HOA "High Overall" Champion, HAA "High All-Around" Champion

35-19   They both put a "death grip" on their shotgun and golf club. Instead hold them gently with no pressure or tension.

35-20   Lower recommended to correct some swing errors that might occur

Questions group 36

36-1 **T or F** In Olympic Trap you move after each shot, not after five shots as in American Trap.

36-2 What year was doubles trap introduced into American Trap tournaments to invigorate the game?

36-3 Which famous London gun maker was known for their "T-shaped" safety?

36-4 A shotgun with the front two inches of the barrel rifled is called what? Who patented this unique feature?

36-5 What is the major criticism of pump shotguns?

36-6 What machining process of a shotgun barrel is supposed to reduce "muzzle jump?"

36-7 **T or F** Screw-in chokes provide no difference to the ideal range or effective range of a shot charge.

36-8 **T or F** Steel shot scores the interior wall of the barrel.

36-9 **T or F** American Trap rules allow one to shoot loads that contain nickel, are copper plated, or tracer loads.

36-10 What is the standard crimp most powder and shotgun shell manufacturers use when conducting pressure tests?

36-11 From what town in England did renowned gun makers supply the prestigious London gun makers?

36-12 When and where was the first recorded use of the term "shotgun?"

36-13 **T or F** Depending on the shooters barrel length, "lead" is learned by mathematical formulas.

36-14 In American Trap, if you are shooting into the wind, blowing toward you, should you hold your shotgun higher or lower?

36-15 What is the correct trap speed for the right target in doubles trap?

36-16 **T or F** If one moves down on the gunstock with his face this will cause tension in the neck muscles, thus causing the shooter to raise his head.

36-17 Name the three time delays that occur during the shooting process.

36-18 _____ is the angle at which the recoil pad sits on your stock to direct recoil. It controls how recoil comes back against your shoulder.

36-19 Black and blue marks after shooting, not located in your shoulder pocket, indicate that what occurred?

36-20 What is the number one safety rule?

Answers group 36

36-1　True. Squads are made up of six shooters moving around five posts.

36-2　1911

36-3　Woodward, and the word "safe" was inlayed gold.

36-4　Paradox, patented by Holland & Holland, 1885

36-5　The time required to work the pump action, and that causes movement of the barrel to fall off the trajectory line.

36-6　Porting – but this question can be argued until the cows come home

36-7　False! A shooter should know both the ideal and the effective range of their chokes.

36-8　False! With the plastic wad used today, the steel shot never touches the inside of the barrel.

36-9　False, a violation of the rules

36-10　0.055″ inches, best between 0.050″ and 0.060″

36-11　Birmingham, England

36-12　1776 in Kentucky, published in *Frontier Language of the West,* by James Fennimore Cooper

36-13　False. Lead is learned by experience!

36-14　Hold higher as the incoming wind will force the bird upwards; a following wind is just the opposite, forcing the bird down.

36-15　39 mph for doubles; singles and handicap 42 mph; 0.5 mph tolerance

36-16　True, and then missing the shot.

36-17　Human reaction time (from brain's decision to fire to pulling the trigger), mechanical delay (firing mechanism to function to muzzle blast) and shot travel (time for shot to hit the target)

36-18　Pitch

36-19　Poor gun mounting!

36-20　There are truly many (get to know them) but, NEVER casually point a shotgun at anyone.

Questions group 37

37-1 _____ _____ is the additional yardage a shooter receives for his high handicap scores in specific shoots, or for his high average at the end of the year.

37-2 **T or F** History shows that the gun engravers in Europe came from gold and silver-smithing trades, while London's engravers came from the printing trades.

37-3 Which choke gives a 70% pattern at the given yardage of 40 yards, 35 yards and 30 yards?

37-4 Who broke the first 200 x 200 singles at The Grand American, the same year Annie Oakley shot?

37-5 Where is the "magazine" located that covers pump and automatic shotguns?

37-6 **T or F** It is strongly suggested by experienced shooters to NOT let new shotgun shooters try "release triggers."

37-7 **T or F** If you mount too low on your shoulder (and lower your face onto the comb) it will not affect your shooting.

37-8 The shotgun nicknamed "The Icon" is manufactured by whom?

37-9 What are the two main factors in shot pattern density?

37-10 **T or F** Gravity can cause a shot cloud drop 3 inches at 40 yards and the shot cloud center by up to 4-5" at 40+ yards.

37-11 **T or F** In Automatic Ball Trap (ABT), there is one trap oscillating horizontally and vertically within a specific range.

37-12 Trap shooters, tennis players, baseball players and golfers must all have what athletic skill?

37-13 What is the most frequently missed American Trap shot?

37-14 Name the three basic rules of etiquette in shotgun sports.

37-15 What type of screwdrivers should be used when working or adjusting your shotgun?

37-16 When was the first "Hand Trap" offered to shooters?

37-17 Acts of Parliament: name the two British Proof Houses authorized by the Gun Barrel Proof Acts.

37-18 **T or F** A barrel that is virtually straight shows its internal reflections as a series of concentric circles.

37-19 If your shotgun hurts your cheek or shoulder, what do you need?

37-20 **T or F** By moving your hand forward or backward on the pistol grip you will feel more difference in your stock than adjusting the trigger.

Answers group 37

37-1   Earned yardage

37-2   True!

37-3   (40 yards) full, (35 yards) modified and (30 yards) improved cylinder

37-4   Steve Crothers, 1925

37-5   Inside the fore-end: the tube below the barrel

37-6   True! New shooters want "to pull" the trigger—it is a safety issue.

37-7   False! It is very easy to lift your head and miss the bird.

37-8   The Parker Gun

37-9   Altitude and air temperature, a third factor that is argued is choke restriction which also affects the pattern density.

37-10   True! Pattern—and study your patterns to have an idea where your shotgun shoots. A 10 mph cross-wind will move your shot string and pattern more than you ever thought.

37-11   True

37-12   Follow-through, keep the shotgun moving and don't stop it after you pull the trigger.

37-13   Straightaway from post three

37-14   Safety (always #1), courtesy and sportsmanship

37-15   Screwdrivers with a narrow slot

37-16   1902, "J.C." Hand Trap, manufactured by Mitchell Mfg. of London, Ohio

37-17   London and Birmingham, England

37-18   True. A bent barrel throws a series of ovals, with long axes in place of the bend.

37-19   A gun fitting because shooting a shotgun is not supposed to hurt.

37-20   True. Trigger adjustment helps with finger comfort.

Questions group 38

38-1　A target released before the shooter calls for it is called what?

38-2　How many optional shots are there in American Trap?

38-3　What type of shotgun barrels are forged by heating narrow strips of iron and steel and shaping them around a mandrel?

38-4　**T or F** Once a barrel reaches a certain "hot" temperature (varies among shotguns) the shotgun will shoot a different point of impact (POI) than when it was cold.

38-5　What are "fliers" in shotgun shooting terms?

38-6　**T or F** Shotgun shooters and rifle shooters should both use a stiff stance in preparing for a shot.

38-7　What is the primary purpose of a shot shell plastic wad?

38-8　What type of shotgun is the most popular today for shooting clay targets?

38-9　What are the ornamental additions to simulate a side-lock shotgun on a box-lock?

38-10　What type of shotgun replaced the lever-action models in popularity?

38-11　**T or F** Patterns at high altitudes are tighter than lower altitudes because of less air resistance.

38-12　What type of choke is used to change the point of impact for patterns that are slightly off center?

38-13　**T or F** Longer barrels have more inertia then shorter ones and will swing faster and steadier.

38-14　Where should one place his finger on the trigger?

38-15　At which trap handicap distance does one need to adjust his gun fit, hold position on the trap house and leads?

38-16　**T or F** Gun sights on the rib help to prevent canting of the shotgun and help to align the dominant eye down the barrel.

38-17　Describe the terms "riding shotgun" and "shotgun wedding."

38-18　What year did clay shooting start with the "luxury class" on board ocean liners?

38-19　When one talks about "small gauge" trap, what gauge would be involved in this new trap game being shot for fun?

38-20　**T or F** On an over/under (O/U) trap gun, the barrels are set as follows: Lower barrel shoots higher and the top barrel shoots flatter.

Answers group 38

38-1 Fast pull!

38-2 None. Skeet has one optional shot.

38-3 Damascus or sometimes called "laminating"

38-4 True!

38-5 Soft lead shot pellets (low antimony) which deform in the barrel causing greater air resistance, loss of velocity speed and they veer off extending the shot string

38-6 False. A shot gunner typically is turning (rotating) during a shot. His shotgun is moving, a rifle is held still.

38-7 The powder wad provides a gas seal and protects the shot, reducing deformation.

38-8 Over & under (O/U), 100 years ago it was the side-by-side double

38-9 Side plates

38-10 Pump shotguns and paper shot shells

38-11 True! Approximately 12% tighter at 5,000 feet vs. sea level

38-12 Offset chokes

38-13 False – longer barrels swing slower

38-14 The trigger is right on the crease between the first and second joint on the forefinger where there is almost no give.

38-15 23-yard line

38-16 True

38-17 This question was for a little fun to break-up the trivia. "Riding Shotgun" means sitting next to the driver and/or you are called the navigator; "shotgun wedding" is a forced marriage due to an unplanned pregnancy.

38-18 1919, when the Volstead Act prohibited drinking "adult beverages" in the United States

38-19 28-gauge

38-20 True, but know your gun by patterning it. The results may be just the opposite or have the same Point of Impact (POI). All shotguns are different!

Questions group 39

39-1 What is the only gauge that is labeled by its bore diameter?

39-2 _____ is an involuntary muscular contraction usually resulting in jerking your shotgun just as it is fired, usually with a missed target resulting.

39-3 What does "service pressure" mean in regards to shotgun terms?

39-4 What was the typical shotgun used by guards on stagecoaches in the 1800s?

39-5 **T or F** An English grip tends to cause the trigger-hand elbow to be held higher, which discourages lifting one's head.

39-6 A trap target, when thrown is broken, or an illegal target in flight, is called what?

39-7 What is a muzzle brake?

39-8 What was the Samurai family name of "SKB?"

39-9 Which of the six following reasons could make your shotgun shoot off center: bent barrel, loose barrel, defective choke tube, choke/barrel alignment, poor gun fit and flinching?

39-10 The shotgun nicknamed "The Basque Beauty" is manufactured by whom?

39-11 **T or F** A soft load in which the shot and wad still leave the gun barrel is called a dud.

39-12 What type of shotgun is not recommended at all for skeet shooting?

39-13 How fast is the velocity in fps of Winchester's AA Trap Target load?

39-14 **T or F** For all International Skeet Tournaments, a shooter may use different types of loads.

39-15 What is the "one thing" that a shooter should start to think about above 3,000 feet elevation?

39-16 At 16-yard American Trap, the barrel width of approximately one inch is equal to how much lead?

39-17 What are the recommended shooting sequences for doubles trap?

39-18 **T or F** In Olympic Trap, it is recommended to shoot chips after a first-shot break.

39-19 **T or F** When the length of your shotgun stock is correct, the tip of your nose should be about an inch from your trigger-hand thumb.

39-20 **T or F** The more ridges you see on a clay target, the less lead required.

Answers group 39

39-1   410

39-2   Flinch

39-3   The top pressure that shot shells cannot exceed, and that all loads must be held below (this pressure level).

39-4   Side-by-side, outside hammers, 20" barrel, 12-gauge

39-5   True, but it still matters how good a shooter you are.

39-6   No-Bird! Called by referee when shooter does not have to fire at the target.

39-7   A recoil reducing device attached to the muzzle

39-8   SAKABA – Drop the three "A"s (vowels) = S K B

39-9   Anyone or any combination of two or more

39-10   Arrizabalaga

39-11   False. It is not a dud. When a portion of the shot load or wad is left in the barrel, then you have a dud.

39-12   Pump - tough to recycle (pump) second shot (too slow) and you would have to readjust your gun mount.

39-13   1325 fps, International Load, 2-3/4″ long, 3-1/4 dram, 24 grams of shot

39-14   False! Only same type of load is allowed.

39-15   Reduced air pressure (altitude), shot string will stay tighter longer than at much lower elevations.

39-16   One barrel width at 16 yards is equal to one foot (12″) lead at the target.

39-17   Straightaway first, then the quartering bird second on each post. Let the arguments begin!

39-18   True. It helps to keep your head down and ensures follow-through.

39-19   True

39-20   True

Questions group 40

40-1 How many targets do men shoot to make up the qualification round in Olympic Trap?

40-2 **T or F** The shooter's eye is the rear sight; a comb too low will cause the shot charge to be below the clay target.

40-3 Name the three non-toxic shot types available today besides steel.

40-4 **T or F** Sparrows at one time replaced pigeons for live bird shoots.

40-5 Normally, about how long does it take to shoot a round of trap and skeet with a full squad of five shooters?

40-6 What was the idea behind release triggers on trap guns?

40-7 The leading hand should be located at a point on the fore-end, at what angle between the elbow and the forearm?

40-8 Which type of shot exerts much more stress on choke tubes, lead or steel?

40-9 Approximately how much recoil should your control hand (the one on the trigger) take and also hold the shotgun in place.

40-10 **T or F** A break-open over and under (O/U) shotgun has shorter overall lengths for the same barrel lengths for pump and automatics.

40-11 The shotgun nicknamed "The Yankee Sidelock" is manufactured by whom?

40-12 What is the most common mistake that shotgun shooters make in shooting clay targets.

40-13 The half pistol, semi-pistol or "bag" grip are commonly called what type of grip today?

40-14 What is a "12-20 Burst?"

40-15 **T or F** It is highly recommended to not use steel shot in side-by-side double shotguns.

40-16 What device measures length of pull, drop at comb and heel, angle of pitch and cast, of any shotgun?

40-17 To help reduce the risk of tick bites (Lyme disease) when shooting, what can you easily do?

40-18 **T or F** Annie Oakley at one time tried trapshooting from an aeroplane.

40-19 **T or F** Moving the cast of a shotgun does not change its center of gravity.

40-20 In American Skeet, when you miss a target the first time, you shoot it again. What target do you want to shoot again?

Answers group 40

40-1   125 targets, then top six shooters shoot an additional 25 targets for final score

40-2   True. If comb is too low, shot will be below target (low); if comb is too high, shot will be above target (high)

40-3   Bismuth, tungsten-matrix and tungsten-polymer

40-4   True, very popular at the Limited Gun Club of Indianapolis, Indiana

40-5   American Trap 12–15 minutes; Skeet 30–35 minutes

40-6   That the shooter would be less likely to flinch on straightaway targets

40-7   90–100 degrees

40-8   Steel, which is much harder than lead, but the plastic wad protects the barrel and choke (open for discussion)

40-9   50%

40-10 True

40-11 L.C. Smith

40-12 Stopping the shotgun (swing) before they actually complete their shot(s). Lifting one's head is also a very good argument.

40-13 "Prince of Wales" grip

40-14 When one mistakenly puts a 20-gauge shot shell in the barrel ahead of a 12-gauge shot shell. VERY unsafe, will destroy the shotgun and could seriously hurt the shooter if fired!

40-15 True! Some instruction manuals say steel is OK!, but be careful and safe at all times.

40-16 The shotgun "Combo Gauge"

40-17 Wear light-colored protective clothing, use insect repellent containing DEET. Wash and check your body and clothing after shooting.

40-18 True (not very successful), and so did some other women try it, also without any luck!

40-19 False. It moves the center of gravity laterally.

40-20 Low #8, which means you got 23 straight birds, missed the 24th and the next target may give you a 24/25 score.

Questions group 41

41-1   Name the five standard clay targets used in sporting clays.

41-2   Where is the National Sporting Clay Association located?

41-3   Which sporting clay games use a "menu card?"

41-4   Describe the flight pattern of a "Springing Teal."

41-5   What does the French word "parcours" mean?

41-6   What is the muzzle constriction called on a shotgun to control shot spread?

41-7   **T or F** The trend in FITASC is to use longer barrel lengths with sporting clay guns.

41-8   **T or F** In sporting clays, you usually shoot the bird that is going to be the most difficult first.

41-9   Which bird presentation in sporting clays is often missed because one shoots at the wrong time?

41-10   What game has replaced or simulates live boxed pigeon shooting?

41-11   At what distance is the American ZZ shooting stand set for targets?

41-12   In FITASC, if both targets are broken by one shot (Annie Oakley) in doubles, how is it scored?

41-13   Describe the "Show Bird."

41-14   **T or F** Many poor shots in sporting clays are caused by a rushed mount, thus losing control of the muzzle(s).

41-15   What is the spot called where the shooter will place his gun before calling for his target in sporting clays?

41-16   **T or F** In sporting clays, you should pre-mount on any shot that you believe is a trap shot.

41-17   Can ZZ birds be used in a FITASC competition?

41-18   What is the worst mistake you can make with your choke selection?

41-19   How many shooting classes are there sporting clays?

41-20   What percentage is recommended for the number of targets in a sporting clays tournament that should be specialty targets, i.e. rabbits, mini, battue, etc.

Answers group 41

41-1   Standard 108mm (pheasant); rabbit 108mm; mini 60mm; midi 90mm; battue 108mm; special flash targets 110mm

41-2   5931 Roft Road, San Antonio, Texas 78253, 210-688-3371

41-3   Sporting Clays and 5-Stand

41-4   Straight up to various heights right in front of the shooter

41-5   A round of FITASC sporting clays – 25 birds

41-6   Choke

41-7   True

41-8   True, but there are exceptions.

41-9   Springing Teal

41-10   ZZ birds, Helice

41-11   30 yards

41-12   "one" and "one"

41-13   A trial throw of the bird(s) you will shoot at that particular station in sporting clays. They are observed but not shot.

41-14   True. A good gun mount is paramount in producing good shots.

41-15   Hold Point

41-16   True

41-17   Yes, adds an interesting feature to the competition.

41-18   Blaming a miss on the choke. (What about your technique and skill in shooting a shotgun?)

41-19   Seven (7) – Master, AA, A, B, C, D and E

41-20   30% to 40%

Questions group 42

42-1   How many shots (targets) consist of a round of 5-Stand?

42-2   In FITASC, what does "Raffael" mean?

42-3   What does "fur & feather" usually mean on a sporting clays course?

42-4   An Anson & Deeley box-lock is identified by what two features?

42-5   Where are most rabbit shots missed?

42-6   Before the ZZ birds, what other invention was similar in a propeller-driven target?

42-7   What is one of the major mistakes in establishing a hold point in sporting clays?

42-8   What is the advantage of holding a low-gun on crossing birds in sporting clays?

42-9   **T or F** In FITASC, both shots can be fired at the same target in doubles.

42-10   Name the three types of pairs used in sporting clays.

42-11   What is the European formula for barrel lengths?

42-12   What is the best grade of wood for gun stocks and fore-ends?

42-13   **T or F** One of the most common mistakes is starting to mount your shotgun with the back hand.

42-14   If the master eye is too high, relative to the breech of the gun, where will your shot go?

42-15   What was the toughest shot you ever had in sporting clays?

42-16   **T or F** In FITASC, no shooting at close range targets (game) because it will be unfit for consumption.

42-17   What deviation percentage is acceptable in your patterns with the choke/shell combination you like to shoot?

42-18   What is the max gauge, lead shot size and shot charge for Helice competitions?

42-19   **T or F** The choke bore constrictions for a 20- and 28-gauge shotgun, for cylinder through extra full, is the same dimension.

42-20   How many square inches in a 30″ diameter circle pattern sheet?

Answers group 42

42-1   25 shots, 25 targets

42-2   Trailing bird on doubles

42-3   A rabbit and a bird combination

42-4   Two pins spanning the width of the action, upon which the sears and hammers rotate

42-5   Over the top! Shoot low and into the dirt!

42-6   Bussey's Gyro Trap, 1872, very popular for several years

42-7   Holding too far back, you end up seeing a blur, then you end up chasing the bird

42-8   Moving the shotgun to your face gives you timing!

42-9   True

42-10   Report Pair, Following Pair and Simultaneous (True Pair)

42-11   40 times the bore diameter

42-12   Exhibition Grade

42-13   True. Start mounting by pushing the front hand toward the target.

42-14   High, conversely too low, shot will also go low

42-15   No wrong answer here, mine was a rabbit, edge-on, going straightaway.

42-16   True

42-17   Within a 5% +/- deviation

42-18   12-gauge, #7-1/2 shot size and only 1 ounce.

42-19   True, as a standard choke bore constriction

42-20   706.50 square inches at 21-1/4″ (half diameter circle). This is the core of your pattern, 353.25 square inches. Study your patterns closely in the core area.

Questions ⬤ group 43

43-1   What does the acronym "FITASC" mean?

43-2   Which format, "new" or "old" is used in the World and European FITASC Championships?

43-3   In sporting clays, what is the tendency of the shooter with incoming birds?

43-4   **T or F** "The only thing that is consistent about shotguns is that very few things are consistent."

43-5   "Single Barrel", "Wipe Your Eye" (a protection shoot), "Quail Covey" and "Bird Box Friendly," are all games in what type of shooting?

43-6   A Class "A" FITASC shooter breaks what percentage or more of targets?

43-7   What shooting method is great for fast targets and close targets in sporting clays?

43-8   What is "Windmilling?"

43-9   In sporting clays with a crossing bird, where do you want your hold point?

43-10 **T or F** In FITASC, only one size shot per shell, no spreaders and no reloads are permitted.

43-11 **T or F** Blow-back (or partially burnt particles of powder) is one major reason to wear eyeglasses.

43-12 If you continue to get hit (smacked) in the cheekbone with your gunstock, what is the problem?

43-13 What happens when you allow a target to get way out ahead of your muzzle?

43-14 **T or F** In FITASC, once a shooter is in the shooting stand they are not allowed to make any changes, i.e. chokes.

43-15 The person who is in charge of setting the layouts in FITASC is called what?

43-16 How much effect does a ported barrel have upon the speed of shot as it exits the muzzle?

43-17 Which shot pellet, lead or steel, patterns better at 40 yards?

43-18 Does a longer forcing cone increase your pattern density?

43-19 What are the three things you must consider on every sporting clay target?

43-20 If you are thinking, "Did I get the right shell in the chamber," "Are my feet right," "What is my score," "Why is that dog barking," "Do I have the right chokes in,"... these are all examples of what?

Answers group 43

43-1   Federation Internationale de Tir Aux Sportives de Chasse

43-2   "New" format, but the "old" is more favored as the purest form

43-3   To mount and start shooting too early! Wait a little longer and you will "kill" more birds.

43-4   Identical shotguns with the same chokes and shells may not pattern alike!

43-5   American ZZ birds – AKA Helice

43-6   80%+ Class A; 60%-80% Class B; 40%-60% Class C

43-7   Maintained lead; sustained lead

43-8   Moving the muzzles(s) above and below the line of sight for the target during the mounting of the shotgun. Both hands should work together for success!

43-9   Approximately in the middle between the trap and the break point

43-10   True. Only 1-1/4 oz. or less, plus #6 to #9-1/2 shot size

43-11   True. Eye and ear protection are mandatory when shooting shotgun sports.

43-12   The comb is too high on the stock.

43-13   You use a fast, violent swing that puts you too far ahead of the target and beyond a correct lead resulting in a missed target.

43-14   True! Know the rules.

43-15   Course designer

43-16   Virtually none, as the port holes are near the end of the barrel

43-17   They both pattern, but steel patterns are better as they are harder and stay round with fewer "flyers" veering off from the shot string.

43-18   Yes, because you have less crushing of the pellets and fewer flyers.

43-19   The angle, the speed and the distance

43-20   Mental interruptions, and you will miss the next target...bet on it!

Questions ⊙ group 44

44-1 **T or F** In the rules of FITASC, you are allowed two shots at singles.

44-2 In FITASC, how far down from the top of your shoulder must the heel of the stock touch the body below a horizontal line?

44-3 **T or F** It is now legal to pre-mount in sporting clays.

44-4 Which bird presentation should be shot fairly quickly up its backside?

44-5 How high is the barrier ring fence in ZZ birds that simulate a live pigeon shoot?

44-6 **T or F** As the altitude of a sporting clays course rises (air less dense) it allows a shot string to stay tighter longer.

44-7 _____ is acoustic equipment triggering the trap to throw a bird at the sound of the shooter's voice.

44-8 **T or F** The general rule in planning your shots in sporting clays with a true pair is to shoot the most difficult bird first.

44-9 Where is the belly and comb nose located on a shotgun?

44-10 Approximately what percentage of shotgun stocks fit the shooter "off the shelf?"

44-11 **T or F** At least four traps are required for each "old" format layout and at least three for each "new" layout in FITASC.

44-12 Describe inletted heel and toe plates.

44-13 In what country were the famous Krupp fluid steel barrels manufactured?

44-14 In any single-shot or break-open action, what is the device called that ejects only the fired cases clear of the breech when the action is opened.

44-15 How many levels of instruction are there to be a fully-certified NSCA instructor?

44-16 Name the type of stock used by many trapshooters that is named after an area where many "live pigeon" shoots where held.

44-17 Do you pattern your shotgun the same for sporting clays and trapshooting?

44-18 In what years was the Victorian or Edwardian shooting time period in the United Kingdom?

44-19 If you have one color lens to pick for your shooting glasses, what color is recommended?

44-20 **T or F** Shotgun powder explodes!

Answers group 44

44-1 True

44-2 25 cm below the top of shoulder, 9.85 inches, let's call it 10 inches to be safe

44-3 True

44-4 "Outgoing," don't let it get out of range, shoot quickly when you have a bird/barrel relationship

44-5 Two feet (24"), just like most live pigeon rings

44-6 True

44-7 Sonopull

44-8 True, but not always. In practice, try both ways to feel more comfortable in competitions.

44-9 Belly, under edge (opposite the comb) on the stock, comb nose is the leading point on the comb approximately where your hand grips the stock.

44-10 8% by several estimates (+/- a percentage)

44-11 True

44-12 A little extra attention to the butt-end of the stock with decorative engraved metal cover plates

44-13 Germany

44-14 Automatic selective ejector

44-15 Three levels; it takes five years and 1,900 hours of teaching

44-16 Monte Carlo

44-17 No! Sporting clays—three or four quick shots from 16 yards; trap—one shot at a time from 40 yards

44-18 1880 to 1910, fabulous shooting experiences! See www.vintagers.org

44-19 Yellow. Start here and add colors for other shooting situations like a background of trees and bushes, and cloudy or sunny days.

44-20 False. It burns very rapidly forming gases that expand and propel the shot down the barrel.

Questions   group 45

45-1   What is the shooting sequence for a round of 5-Stand?

45-2   Describe a typical "flight pattern" of a rabbit target.

45-3   **T or F** FITASC targets are all 110m standard clays.

45-4   What is meant by "trajectory?"

45-5   Which lead? You start with the barrel on the target, pull out in front of it, obtain your lead and pull the trigger.

45-6   When should a battue target be shot?

45-7   During the mounting process of the shotgun, what does the forward hand control?

45-8   **T or F** Your weight should be on the ball of your front foot.

45-9   As a sporting clay shooter, how much of the pattern do you want above the bullseye?

45-10   **T or F** In sporting clays, a single target may be shot at twice and scored dead if broken by either shot.

45-11   When one speaks of 45 degree canted recoil pads, what do the pads offer the shooter?

45-12   What is a grip cap?

45-13   What kind of doubles is thrown from the same trap, on the same trajectory, at the reloading sequence of the arm of the trap?

45-14   "_____ _____" shotgun refers to a side-by-side double barrel shotgun with exposed hammers.

45-15   What is the proper head movement during a move, mount and swing shooting presentation?

45-16   **T or F** Our emotions are more influenced by what we hear than what we see.

45-17   **T or F** In Helice, if the referee declares a "no bird!" the shooter shall reload and shoot only one shell at the repeat target.

45-18   **T or F** In Helice, the shooter must say "ready," operator replies "ready," then the shooter calls "pull" and the target is released instantly.

45-19   The most commonly requested barrel length for a side-by-side is 28″ long. What length did famous shooting instructor Robert Churchill recommend?

45-20   Which shotgun sport is designed to imitate the flush of frightened wild bobwhites?

Answers group 45

45-1   Each station, two-shot single targets, report pair and true pair

45-2   On the ground, it rolls, skips, bounces in irregular paths, a "squirrel" target only rolls!

45-3   False – minis, rockets, rabbits and battues are used

45-4   The line followed in space by a target

45-5   Pull-away

45-6   When it slows down at its apex, turns and presents a full body before dropping rapidly

45-7   The muzzle of the shotgun, vertical and horizontal movement

45-8   True. About 60%. Your stance is extremely important! Remember to keep it comfortable.

45-9   You want a 50%/50% pattern; same as a skeet shotgun choke pattern

45-10   True

45-11   Easier shouldering of the shotgun from the "low gun" position

45-12   A protective cover (cap) placed on the end of a grip, i.e. pistol grip, often made with the owner's initials.

45-13   Rafale Double (see FITASC rules on simultaneous doubles)

45-14   Rabbit ears

45-15   Head up, slight head movement forward, as you raise the stock up to your cheek

45-16   True. It's tough to control your emotions when hearing negative or bothersome noises, always important when shooting a 100 straight

45-17   True

45-18   True. This is the correct sequence of "calls."

45-19   25″ long, but the trend is longer than 28″

45-20   Crazy Quail; we need a lot more of these layouts in the United States!

Questions ⬤ group 46

46-1   What is one of the best advantages 5-Stand has over sporting clays for a gun club owner?

46-2   Name the eight target flight paths in 5-Stand.

46-3   In what two countries was FITASC conceived and then developed into a shotgunning sport?

46-4   What is the cartridge load restricted to in FITASC?

46-5   In FITASC, if a clay target is not thrown from the correct trap, how is it scored?

46-6   Which shotgun shooting sport has a "Baulk" rule?

46-7   In what country did sporting clays have its beginning?

46-8   Which shooting method is suggested for a following true pair presentation?

46-9   **T or F** In FITASC, you cannot practice your gun mount at any time after the shooting has commenced.

46-10   Where is the United States Helice Association headquarters located?

46-11   What is the name of the sighting plane affixed along the length of a shotgun barrel with gaps or slots, milled for cooling purposes?

46-12   Which hand brings the shotgun up to your face when you have a proper stance.

46-13   **T or F** A shot string stays the same in hot weather vs. cooler weather.

46-14   Why should a shooter aim or align the pointing finger of the forward hand on the fore-end?

46-15   Among his many inventions for shotguns, which one was Frederick Beesley most famous for?

46-16   **T or F** It is OK to shoot your shotgun without putting in your screw-in chokes.

46-17   **T or F** In FITASC, the shooter must fire with their shotguns shouldered on all targets.

46-18   In a five-machine and a seven-machine Helice layout, how far apart are the machines?

46-19   Who are the only two shotgun manufacturers in the world today that produce side-lock shotguns completely in-house?

46-20   What is the notch called that is cut into the lump or barrel extension into which a bolt enters?

Answers group 46

46-1   A sporting clays experience in a small amount of space; often on a combo skeet and trap field

46-2   Crossers and Quartering (L to R, R to L), Vertical (Teal), Rabbit, Tower (going away, incoming)

46-3   Conceived in Spain, developed in France

46-4   28 grams

46-5   NO Bird

46-6   Helice referee calls it if shooter is disturbed by a spectator or competitor

46-7   England, and then spread to the United States in the 1970s

46-8   Follow-through. Shoot the back bird first, follow-through and shoot the lead bird, always moving the shotgun on the bird trajectory.

46-9   True

46-10   10701 CR 1200, Malakoff, Texas 75148, Phone 817-233-1025

46-11   Ventilated Rib

46-12   Rear hand

46-13   False. In cooler weather the shot strings opens up more.

46-14   It rotates your arm slightly outward making the swinging of the shotgun easier.

46-15   The Purdey Side-lock

46-16   False. Never fire your shotgun without a screw-in choke in place.

46-17   True

46-18   Five machine 4.5 meters minimum to 5 meters max apart; seven machine 3.3 meters apart, evenly spaced

46-19   Merkel, Suhl, Germany and Connecticut Shotgun A-10, New Britain, CT

46-20   Bites

Questions group 47

47-1   What is considered the ultimate prize(s) in clay target shooting sports?

47-2   How many traps are usually used in a 5-Stand course?

47-3   How is a patterning plate different than a patterning paper sheet target with a 30″ diameter circle?

47-4   What happens to a shot string when the shotgun is moving (swinging)?

47-5   What is the angle of the butt, in relation to the top of the barrel, called?

47-6   What is usually the easiest target in sporting clays, but also easy to miss?

47-7   Name the two components that make up the Helice bird.

47-8   What are the two most popular "mount and swing" methods for shooting sporting clays?

47-9   How big are shooting stands for FITASC?

47-10   **T of F** In FITASC, dead targets are scored as "one." While missed targets are scored as "zero."

47-11   What is the best break point for long crossing targets?

47-12   **T or F** Longer forcing cones and recoil pads both reduce recoil.

47-13   Name the three moving parts in an Anson & Deeley lock mechanism.

47-14   What is the fastest growing segment of sporting clays, and which shooting game is more difficult, sporting clays or FITASC?

47-15   In FITASC, one cannot move his gun from his "low-gun" position until what happens?

47-16   In Helice, the barrier ring must be a maximum of how many meters from the machine and how long is the shooting walk?

47-17   **T or F** Coaching a shooter is allowed in FITASC between shots in a station.

47-18   How many shots does a shooter get in Helice to separate the cap ("witness") from the wing?

47-19   Chokes have two functions, one is to shape the shot pattern, what is the other function?

47-20   Gunsmith vs. gunmaker, describe the difference.

Answers group 47

47-1   The European and World FITASC Cup Titles (this one you can argue until the cows come home!)

47-2   Six to eight traps, but only five shooting stands

47-3   For testing sporting clays, the plate is painted or greased and one shoots standing, free style, to find their impact point.

47-4   The shot string becomes oblong and elliptical in shape.

47-5   Pitch

47-6   Incomer. Take your time—when it is slow, fat and is showing its underside belly, pull the trigger.

47-7   Propeller (aka, wing or prop) and the cap (aka, witness cap)

47-8   The Churchill Mount; the Stanbury Mount

47-9   One meter square or one meter diameter circle

47-10   True

47-11   Best break point is just after it reaches its apex

47-12   True

47-13   The tumbler (or hammer), sear and the cocking dog. The dog cocks the tumbler, the sear holds it in place and the trigger releases it.

47-14   Women shooters are the fastest growing segment; FITASC is absolutely the more difficult game.

47-15   Until the requested target is visible.

47-16   21 meters for barrier ring; shooting walk 24 meters minimum to 30 meters

47-17   False!

47-18   Two shots, just like in live pigeons.

47-19   They separate the shot cup (wad) from the shot.

47-20   Gun maker: the one whose name appears on the shotgun and is apprenticed as a gunsmith; i.e. a shotgun barrel-maker would be a gunsmith.

Questions group 48

48-1   How many targets make up a round of FITASC?

48-2   **T or F** In FITASC, doubles are previewed unless they are Report Pairs of the singles already previewed and shot.

48-3   What is a "Cheek Piece?"

48-4   What is the distance from the top of the barrel or rib to the top edge of the stock at the comb and the heel called?

48-5   **T or F** In sporting clays, many experts suggest one use the same chokes in an over and under (O/U), which eliminates concerns about switching barrels.

48-6   At what point do many experts suggest you shoot at a springing teal?

48-7   **T or F** 12-gauge shot gunners are subject to impact noise of 140dB (decibels), which is a highly damaging noise level.

48-8   What is the only shot one should take when your nose is not over your toes (weight on back feet)?

48-9   **T or F** In hot and warm weather, you want tighter chokes (patterns); in cold and dry weather you want open chokes (patterns) to be able to break targets at desired distances.

48-10   What is the maximum time allowed to a shooter between single or double targets in FITASC?

48-11   How many pairs of "Show Birds" may be viewed at each station in sporting clays?

48-12   Who has greater eye dominance problems, men or women?

48-13   What problem does wrong finger placement on the trigger cause?

48-14   What is the "angle of pitch" on a shotgun?

48-15   Name the two types of crimps found on shot shells.

48-16   If a gun fitter asks you what you would like to have done, what should you answer?

48-17   What length is regarded as the best length for a forcing cone that has also been honed and burnished?

48-18   **T or F** In Helice, to score a "Good", the white center cap of the Helice must be completely separate from the orange wing and fall inside the ring.

48-19   What should not be part of a Helice ring? Level ground, shooting north or northeast with axis through the shooting stand, and middle machine.

48-20   **T or F** Canting a shotgun will cause the shooter to shoot lower and the center of the pattern will go to the side canted.

Answers group 48

48-1   25 – a course is called a "parcours" or layout. A competition can vary in the number of "parcours" shot.

48-2   True

48-3   A raised area, usually on custom stocks to fit a shooter's cheek.

48-4   Drop

48-5   True, so there is no mental interruption worrying about chokes causing missed shots.

48-6   At the apex (the top), when the bird has virtually stopped before it starts to fall.

48-7   True! Hearing loss is absolutely irreparable.

48-8   High incoming birds

48-9   True. Remember to pattern your chokes and shotguns in all types of weather conditions.

48-10   Twenty seconds

48-11   One show pair. Only the first person in the squad to shoot this station may mount his unloaded shotgun and track the targets.

48-12   Women, but men are more often color blind

48-13   Timing – throws it off just slightly enough that you miss the bird

48-14   The angle at which the shotgun butt stock fits your shoulder (pocket)

48-15   "Folded Crimp" popular in America, "Rolled Crimp" found in British and European cartridges

48-16   Ask to check this fitter's credentials, he may not be a real gun fitter at all!

48-17   Many experts state 1-1/2″ is best

48-18   True

48-19   All OK and part of the standard Helice ring

48-20   True

Questions group 49

49-1   How soon after a referee's call must a bird be thrown in FITASC?

49-2   Name the four types of shots you'll experience in a round of sporting clays.

49-3   **T or F** A popular tip for shooting rabbits is to close one's left eye (R/H shooter) and shoot right at the rabbit.

49-4   How many malfunctions is a sporting clays shooter allowed per day, per event, attributed to gun or ammunition malfunction?

49-5   **T or F** Like sporting clays, chokes may be changed between stations in 5-Stand.

49-6   **T or F** High-pressured shot shells will result in greater deformation of the shot pellet and wider spreads beyond the muzzle.

49-7   In "old" FITASC, the traps are marked ___ ___ ___ ___ and the shooting stands are marked ___ ___ ___ ___.

49-8   Do all of the products offered to protect a shooter's ear (hearing) work properly and do a good job?

49-9   Rose & Scroll and ornamental scroll are examples of what, and from what country?

49-10   **T or F** Both shots must be fired during the acceleration phase of the flight of the Helice target.

49-11   **T or F** A left-handed shooter that is right eye dominant will miss to the right of the target.

49-12   What target is 28 cms overall, weights 70 grams, has a top part that is 10.4 cms in diameter and comes in various colors.

49-13   Should a battue be shot before or after it starts to fall?

49-14   What type of chokes and shells are suggested for Helice shooting?

49-15   When cleaning your shotgun barrel, do you clean from the breech to the muzzle or in the opposite direction?

49-16   Trapshooters like a pattern 60/40 percent, because the target is always rising. What percentage pattern do a lot of sporting clay shooter like?

49-17   What choke and shot size is recommended for close range rabbit shots (10 to 20 yards)?

49-18   What shotgun book (actually 3 volumes) is considered the "best," a must-have for a collection?

49-19   **T or F** In sporting clays, a shooter should keep his barrels below the line of the target until he sees the target and then comes up through the line to the target.

49-20   Shooting with both eyes open, what does the non-master eye provide for the shooter?

Answers group 49

49-1   Three seconds or less

49-2   Singles, simultaneous doubles, report pair (doubles) and following doubles

49-3   True!

49-4   Three

49-5   False, no choke changing after the round has started

49-6   True

49-7   A - B - C - D; Stand 1, Stand 2, Stand 3 and Stand 4

49-8   NO! A shooter should be aware of this fact and spend the time to get correct-fitting hearing protection. Invest in good ear protection, not lowest price!

49-9   Engraving, made famous by English gun engravers

49-10 True

49-11 True! The opposite set-up, miss to the left of the target.

49-12 A Helice target

49-13 Before, because it falls very quickly and moves forward very little—hard to track!

49-14 Tight chokes with 1-1/4 ounce shot shells; "visible piece" does not count, there must be separation.

49-15 Always clean breech to muzzle with patches and bore brush

49-16 50/50 percent because of the variety of shots

49-17 Open as you can get chokes; cylinder or skeet, 1-1/8 oz. of #9 shot

49-18 *The Modern Shotgun* by Major Sir Gerald Burrard

49-19 True

49-20 Peripheral vision and depth perception to judge distance and size of the target

Questions 🎯 group 50

50-1   **T or F** In FITASC, two shooters in the same squad are not permitted to use or share the same shotgun in an official competition or championship.

50-2   **T or F** Target trajectory is more important than lead on a rapidly dropping target.

50-3   What is the number one key to good consistent shotgun shooting?

50-4   When shooting doubles in sporting clays, if you rush your swing on the first bird, what will probably happen on the second bird?

50-5   In "Wipe Your Eye," how many targets are thrown for the two shooters?

50-6   **T or F** A shooter in sporting clays cannot use a marker (like some landscape feature) to set a hold point.

50-7   What little trick do expert shooters use with rabbits to increase their kill rate?

50-8   **T or F** The master eye puts the muzzle into the right position (relationship) with the clay bird, thus the shot goes where the shooter is looking.

50-9   What was the toughest shot you ever had to shoot in FITASC?

50-10 **T or F** In FITASC, a contestant does not necessarily have to shoot at each single target.

50-11 What is the shooting order in "old" style FITASC?

50-12 Is a polychoke a good choice for sporting clays?

50-13 **T or F** Both box-locks and side-locks utilize a "Scott Spindle" that holds the lever, so it can open and close the shotgun.

50-14 At what distance should Helice shooters start and then slide back one meter for each break of five consecutive targets on a seven-box ring, and three targets on a five-box ring? Maximum is 30-meter mark.

50-15 For all competitive shooting sports with referees, what is the one best thing a competitor should do before shooting at an event or tournament?

50-16 What is the most controversial style of shotgun shooting?

50-17 Name the three minimum measurements to have a 5-Stand layout.

50-18 How many fingers should a shooter place between his nose and the ends of his fingers on the stock grip?

50-19 Name the common choke restrictions for the following chokes: Skeet, IC, Mod and Full.

50-20 What is the rare and elusive "Swedish Mistress" in sporting clays?

Answers group 50

50-1   True

50-2   True

50-3   Proper gun fit

50-4   You would lose your balance and timing (no rhythm) and most likely miss the second bird

50-5   Three birds – calls for instinctive response and teamwork between the two shooters

50-6   False. Use a tree, bush, cactus, building, telephone pole—I have even used clouds.

50-7   Shoot into the ground ahead of the rabbit and use the dirt, stones, gravel, whatever, to increase your shot string density.

50-8   True, this is why proper gun fit is so very important.

50-9   Springing teal battue with only its edge-on exposed. I missed half of them! Tough shot!

50-10   False – just the opposite

50-11   First shooter (squad leader) shoots single target, then after squad is finished, the second shooter starts off the double followed by the rest of the squad

50-12   It is OK and fun to use and try, but with screw-in chokes today, a polychoke's popularity wanes

50-13   True

50-14   27-meter mark

50-15   Read, understand and know the rules well—it will help your shooting experience.

50-16   The Churchill Method. People argue about it all the time.

50-17   50 yards wide at shooting stand, 300-yard shot fall-out and 80 degrees arc for safe shot fall

50-18   Two fingers – an American style measurement

50-19   Skeet .005; IC .010; Modified .020; Full .035

50-20   I don't know, never could find the correct answer. Maybe reason enough for another trivia book.

McGuire's No-Nonsense Target Shotgun Safety Rules

SAFETY FIRST AND ALWAYS!

As a shotgun owner and/or shotgun shooter, you accept all the demanding responsibilities of shotgun safety. These responsibilities are very important and can mean the difference between serious injury or death to yourself or others. The failure to respect the following safety rules can cause extensive damage to your shotgun, and again, disastrous results to you and those around you.

There are NO excuses for careless or abusive handling of any shotgun. You must, at all times, respect the power and potential danger of a shotgun. Read and learn the following rules for shotgun safety before you start to fire a shotgun. Ask questions and discuss the safety rules with experienced shotgun shooters if you do not understand any of the rules. An appreciation of the safety rules will enhance your shotgun shooting experience. Do not be timid when it comes to shotgun safety!

1. NEVER, EVER point a shotgun (muzzle) at another person or in any unsafe direction!

2. Always make sure your shotgun is unloaded when handling it with others or preparing to clean it. ACTION OPEN!

3. Beware of what mechanical "safety" devices truly mean. Never rely totally on "safeties," as they are mechanical devices, and they can fail!

4. Never transport your shotgun when it is loaded! Always store your shotgun in an unloaded condition and separate from any ammunition!

5. Make sure your barrel(s) has NO obstructions. When checking, make sure the shotgun is fully unloaded!

6. Always handle all shotguns with the respect due a loaded and ready-to-fire shotgun! Do not fire the firing pin on an empty chamber. It might not be empty!

7. Always make sure the shot shell is the correct one for the gauge of your shotgun and the correct length! Store different gauge shot shells in labeled separate containers; never mix shot shell gauges!

8. Without exception, always wear eye and ear protection when shotgun shooting!

9. Never mix shotgun shooting activities with alcoholic beverages or any type of drugs before or during a shoot!

10. Keep your fingers away from the trigger when unloading or loading your shotgun until you are ready to shoot!

11. Always be aware of your surrounding shooters. Be defensive and on guard against unsafe shotgun handling. If violations are occurring of any safety rules, politely suggest safer handling procedures!

12. If your shotgun fails to fire, keep the muzzle pointed downrange in a safe direction!

13. Always be aware of the signs of a shot shell malfunction. If you detect any off sound or feel light recoil when a shot shell is fired, do not load another shell until properly checking your shotgun!

14. Do not alter the trigger, safety or other parts of the firing mechanism of your shotgun under any circumstances!

15. Talk up shotgun safety at all times to all members of your family and friends. Teach and supervise shotgun safety to new shooters, non-shooters and especially children!

SAFETY FIRST AND ALWAYS!

NOTES

NOTES